ADULT DEPARTMENT
JULIUS FORSTMANN LIBRARY
PUBLIC LIBRARY
UE
07055

D0386483

821.1

E 51940

PASSAIC PUBLIC LIBRARY, NJ

3 2344 05042275 1

DATE DUE

THE CANTERBURY TALES

OTHER TITLES IN THE GREENHAVEN PRESS
LITERARY COMPANION SERIES:

AMERICAN AUTHORS

Nathaniel Hawthorne
Ernest Hemingway
Herman Melville
Arthur Miller
John Steinbeck
Mark Twain

BRITISH AUTHORS

Jane Austen

WORLD AUTHORS

Sophocles

BRITISH LITERATURE

Shakespeare: The Comedies
Shakespeare: The Sonnets
Shakespeare: The Tragedies

THE GREENHAVEN PRESS
Literary Companion
TO BRITISH LITERATURE

THE CANTERBURY TALES

David Bender, *Publisher*
Bruno Leone, *Executive Editor*
Scott Barbour, *Managing Editor*
Bonnie Szumski, *Series Editor*
Don Nardo, *Book Editor*

ADULT DEPARTMENT
JULIUS FORSTMANN LIBRARY
PASSAIC PUBLIC LIBRARY
195 GREGORY AVENUE
PASSAIC, NEW JERSEY 07055

Greenhaven Press, San Diego, CA

Library of Congress Cataloging-in-Publication Data

Readings on the canterbury tales / Don Nardo, book editor.
        p.   cm. — (Greenhaven Press literary companion
to British literature)
    Includes bibliographical references and index.
    ISBN 1-56510-586-9 (lib. : alk. paper). —
ISBN 1-56510-585-0 (pbk. : alk. paper)
    1. Chaucer, Geoffrey, d. 1400. Canterbury tales. 2.
Christian pilgrims and pilgrimages in literature. 3. Tales,
Medieval—History and criticism. I. Nardo, Don, 1947–   .
II. Series.
PR1874.R43   1997
821'.1–dc20   96-21136
                                                                    CIP

Cover photo: © Bettmann

No part of this book may be reproduced or used in any
form or by any means, electrical, mechanical, or otherwise,
including, but not limited to, photocopy, recording, or any
information storage and retrieval system, without prior
written permission from the publisher.
    Every effort has been made to trace the owners of
copyrighted material.

Copyright ©1997 by Greenhaven Press, Inc.
PO Box 289009
San Diego, CA 92198-9009
Printed in the U.S.A.

> *In Southwark, at the Tabard*
>   *as I lay*
> *Ready to wend on my pilgrimage*
> *To Canterbury with a fully*
>   *devout heart,*
> *At night there came into that inn*
> *Full nine and twenty in a*
>   *company,*
> *Of sundry folk, by chance fallen*
> *Into fellowship, and pilgrims*
>   *were they all,*
> *That toward Canterbury would*
>   *ride.*

**Geoffrey Chaucer,
from the General Prologue to
*The Canterbury Tales***

CONTENTS

ficult for the uninitiated; hence the many modern translations of his works. However, a little patient study of how
the words, pronunciations, and rhythms of the English
language have changed over the centuries rewards the
reader with the ability to understand and enjoy Chaucer's
lines exactly as he wrote them.

Chapter Two: Important Themes in
The Canterbury Tales

Chapter Three: Specific Characters and Stories in *The Canterbury Tales*

tell two ludicrous and inept stories. The real Chaucer was
far from inept, of course, as his clever use of the *Tale of
Melibeus* shows.

FOREWORD

*"'Tis the good reader that
makes the good book."*

Ralph Waldo Emerson

The story's bare facts are simple: The captain, an old and scarred seafarer, walks with a peg leg made of whale ivory. He relentlessly drives his crew to hunt the world's oceans for the great white whale that crippled him. After a long search, the ship encounters the whale and a fierce battle ensues. Finally the captain drives his harpoon into the whale, but the harpoon line catches the captain about the neck and drags him to his death.

A simple story, a straightforward plot—yet, since the 1851 publication of Herman Melville's *Moby-Dick*, readers and critics have found many meanings in the struggle between Captain Ahab and the whale. To some, the novel is a cautionary tale that depicts how Ahab's obsession with revenge leads to his insanity and death. Others believe that the whale represents the unknowable secrets of the universe and that Ahab is a tragic hero who dares to challenge fate by attempting to discover this knowledge. Perhaps Melville intended Ahab as a criticism of Americans' tendency to become involved in well-intentioned but irrational causes. Or did Melville model Ahab after himself, letting his fictional character express his anger at what he perceived as a cruel and distant god?

Although literary critics disagree over the meaning of *Moby-Dick*, readers do not need to choose one particular interpretation in order to gain an understanding of Melville's novel. Instead, by examining various analyses, they can gain numerous insights into the issues that lie under the surface of the basic plot. Studying the writings of literary critics can also aid readers in making their own assessments of *Moby-Dick* and other literary works and in developing analytical thinking skills.

The Greenhaven Literary Companion Series was created with these goals in mind. Designed for young adults, this unique anthology series provides an engaging and comprehensive introduction to literary analysis and criticism. The essays included in the Literary Companion Series are chosen for their accessibility to a young adult audience and are expertly edited in consideration of both the reading and comprehension levels of this audience. In addition, each essay is introduced by a concise summation that presents the contributing writer's main themes and insights. Every anthology in the Literary Companion Series contains a varied selection of critical essays that cover a wide time span and express diverse views. Wherever possible, primary sources are represented through excerpts from authors' notebooks, letters, and journals and through contemporary criticism.

Each title in the Literary Companion Series pays careful consideration to the historical context of the particular author or literary work. In-depth biographies and detailed chronologies reveal important aspects of authors' lives and emphasize the historical events and social milieu that influenced their writings. To facilitate further research, every anthology includes primary and secondary source bibliographies of articles and/or books selected for their suitability for young adults. These engaging features make the Greenhaven Literary Companion series ideal for introducing students to literary analysis in the classroom or as a library resource for young adults researching the world's great authors and literature.

Exceptional in its focus on young adults, the Greenhaven Literary Companion Series strives to present literary criticism in a compelling and accessible format. Every title in the series is intended to spark readers' interest in leading American and world authors, to help them broaden their understanding of literature, and to encourage them to formulate their own analyses of the literary works that they read. It is the editors' hope that young adult readers will find these anthologies to be true companions in their study of literature.

INTRODUCTION

The essays selected for the Greenhaven Literary Companion to *The Canterbury Tales* provide students and teachers with a wide range of information and opinion about Geoffrey Chaucer's masterpiece. These selections were chosen and organized for readers who have never before read or studied the *Tales* or any other works by Chaucer. To the uninitiated, Chaucer's archaic style, language, and descriptions can at first glance appear strange and intimidating; however, aided by this comprehensive and easy-to-read introductory volume, as well as a little patience, many readers will likely find *The Canterbury Tales* humorous, entertaining, and surprisingly easy to understand.

The unusual clarity and usefulness of this literary companion volume is partly facilitated by a division of the essays into three sections ranging from the general to the specific. The first section contains selections dealing with Chaucer's language and the overall conception and construction of *The Canterbury Tales*. One selection, for example, explores the author's original concept of the general structure of this massive, unfinished work and speculates about the missing pieces. Another selection discusses how the Middle English wording and style of the author's verse, which was perfectly understandable in his day, became increasingly difficult to read and understand as the language continued to evolve in succeeding centuries. And still another selection examines how Chaucer conceived and used the device of a narrator in structuring the *Tales*.

The second section features essays dealing with the major themes of *The Canterbury Tales*. In one of the most important and often quoted of the thousands of modern studies of the *Tales*, a famous Chaucerian scholar explores how Chaucer developed and utilized the theme of marriage in the work. Other selections focus on romance, religion, technology, and other recurring themes. As the essays reveal, the range and interpretation of these themes are still hotly debated by scholars.

The last section contains selections dealing with specific characters from *The Canterbury Tales* and the individual stories they tell in the course of their journey to Canterbury cathedral. The Knight, the Prioress, the Miller, and the Pardoner, among the most famous and widely discussed of these pilgrims, are each the subject of a penetrating essay by a highly regarded scholar. Additional selections examine less popular but no less literarily fascinating characters, including Sir Thopas and Melibeus, the subjects of the often overlooked tales told by the narrator, the pilgrim character identified with Chaucer himself.

All of the essays in this collection were written by English professors at leading colleges and universities, scholars of medieval history or literature, or scholars specializing in Chaucer and his works. Many of those Chaucerian experts still living regularly publish new articles and essays that explore or debate ideas, issues, literary techniques, and characters in *The Canterbury Tales* and other writings by Chaucer. One of their most prestigious outlets is the quarterly journal *The Chaucer Review*, produced by the Pennsylvania State University Press, a publication from which some of the essays in this collection were taken.

The Literary Companion to Chaucer's *Canterbury Tales* has several special features. Each of the essays explains or discusses in detail a specific, narrowly focused topic. The introduction to each essay sums up the main points so that the reader knows what to expect. Interspersed within the essays, the reader will discover inserts that serve as examples of ideas expressed by the authors, offer supplementary information, and/or add authenticity and color. These inserts are drawn from various translations of *The Canterbury Tales*, from critical commentary about that work, or from other scholarly sources.

GEOFFREY CHAUCER: A BIOGRAPHY

CHAUCER AND *THE CANTERBURY TALES*

In 1400, the English poet Geoffrey Chaucer died, leaving his most comprehensive and ambitious literary effort, *The Canterbury Tales*, unfinished. In fact, the parts of the work Chaucer did finish represent less than a quarter of what he originally intended; of well over one hundred projected tales, he completed only twenty-one. And yet, this fragment of what might have been encompasses some seventeen thousand lines of verse and presents, in deft, witty, penetrating, and stunningly detailed descriptions, an almost unparalleled panorama of everyday life and thinking in the Late Middle Ages.

In particular, Chaucer's artful travelogue of a group of religious pilgrims marching toward Canterbury cathedral captures the appearances, habits, attitudes, and beliefs of people of all social classes of the period. "The descriptions of the various pilgrims," remarks former New York University scholar and Chaucer translator Vincent Hopper,

> turn in rapid sequence from an article of clothing to a point of character and back again with no apparent organization or desire for it. Yet so effective is this artful artlessness that each pilgrim stands out sharply as a type of medieval personality and also as a highly individualized character. . . . As a result, *The Canterbury Tales* is a vivacious [lively] picture of the Middle Ages and an eternally alive gallery of humanity.

Christopher Baswell, assistant professor of English at Barnard College, echoes this view of Chaucer's amazing gift for characterization, saying that the *Tales* constitutes

> perhaps the richest, fullest portrait of a world and its people ever achieved by any writer. From the restraint and grandeur of his Knight to the flashy idiom and broad humor of his Wife of Bath, from the fairy-tale setting of the Franklin's Tale to the barnyard reality of the Nun's Priest's Tale, Chaucer's range of characterization and tone is unparalleled.

Considering the great scope and quality of the existing sections of *The Canterbury Tales*, it is tantalizing to imagine the literary heights the work might have attained if Chaucer had found the time to finish it. Had he been a full-time poet and artist, perhaps he would have done so; however, for the better part of his adult life he was occupied with the many duties that attended his jobs as civil servant and diplomat to the English royal court and government. That he was only a part-time writer makes his literary achievements, especially his masterpiece, *The Canterbury Tales*, all the more extraordinary.

TAKING ADVANTAGE OF FAMILY CONNECTIONS

In a way, practically everything Chaucer did in his life helped prepare him for writing his masterpiece. Though he lived only about sixty years, those years were busy and eventful and his experiences, both professional and personal, brought him into contact with diverse types of people from all walks of life. Gifted with keen powers of observation and a near photographic memory, he stored away innumerable portraits of character types, individuals, and personalities that would eventually spill out onto the pages of *The Canterbury Tales*.

Little is known about Geoffrey Chaucer's childhood. He was born sometime between 1340 and 1343, probably in London, to a well-to-do family headed by John Chaucer, a wine importer, and his wife, Agnes. Both John and his own father had connections at England's royal court, over which members of the noble Lancaster family had held considerable influence since the preceding century. Taking advantage of these connections, young Geoffrey's father and grandfather periodically held court offices, in which capacity they met and did favors for many of the most prominent families of English society. Collecting a few favors in return from well-placed individuals, John Chaucer was able to provide his son with the best educational experiences then possible for a commoner. About 1349, for instance, Geoffrey began attending London's prestigious Saint Paul's Cathedral School. Later, in 1357, the younger Chaucer served as a page in the household of Lionel, earl of Ulster, and his wife, Countess Elizabeth. Through these and presumably other similar experiences, the young man learned Latin and French, the rules of courtly behavior, and how to bear arms and fight for the king. And fight he did. In 1359 and 1360 he served in the

English army, which was then engaged in France in the first phase of the so-called Hundred Years' War, a long on-again, off-again conflict between the two nations.

After being captured and then ransomed, Chaucer returned to England. There, evidence suggests, he studied law and finance and began serving periodically as a diplomat for the government. Utilizing his connections as his father and grandfather had, he increasingly attached himself to the royal court and the nobles who attended it. In 1366, Chaucer married Philippa Roet, a lady-in-waiting to Queen Philippa, a union arranged by the queen herself. And the following year King Edward III formally drafted the young man into the service of the royal household, awarding him a generous annual salary for life. In the ensuing years, Chaucer faithfully earned that salary in numerous government positions, including, in addition to his continuing diplomatic duties, Esquire of the Royal Household (in which he arranged court functions and entertained guests) and Comptroller of Customs.

CHAUCER'S FIRST LITERARY EFFORTS

It was also during these young adult years that Chaucer first began writing poetry. At the time, he probably did not appreciate that while his busy professional duties limited the size of his literary output they also brought him into contact with a wide range of character types that he would later incorporate into his works. As medieval scholar Marchette Chute explains:

> The one disadvantage of Chaucer's career as a civil servant was that it naturally did not give him much time for writing. But to balance this he had not only financial independence but also an opportunity to meet all sorts and conditions of people. Chaucer had his share of office work as Comptroller of the Customs and as Clerk of the Works [to which he was appointed in 1389; the job entailed maintaining the palace, the Tower of London, and other government buildings], but even in these positions he was in contact with a great variety of human beings, from wool merchants to masons and from highway robbers to shipmen. He was in close contact throughout the whole of his career with the brilliant international courts of two kings, and his work as a diplomat brought him in[to] contact not only with the culture of France but with the new poetry that was flowering on the other side of the Alps. If Chaucer's career as a civil servant had done nothing more than send him to Italy, it would have been worth it to him.

Indeed, Chaucer's early works are heavily influenced by his French and Italian literary contemporaries. In what is now frequently referred to as his French period, ending around 1372, he worked at translating popular French works, wrote some short poems in French, and also composed *The Book of the Duchess*, a thirteen-hundred-line poem eulogizing Lady Blanche, wife of John of Gaunt, son of the king and a nobleman close to the Chaucer family. In the next decade, his so-called Italian period, Chaucer became increasingly productive. He turned out several long works, including *The House of Fame*, influenced by the *Divine Comedy* of the Italian poet Dante; *The Parliament of Fowls*; and *Troilus and Criseyde*.

Troilus and Criseyde is universally recognized as the greatest of these works, and most critics consider it Chaucer's finest writing after *The Canterbury Tales*. *Troilus*'s 8,239 lines of verse describe an episode from the famous Trojan War, originally recounted by the ancient Greek bard Homer in his epic poem the *Iliad*. While the Greeks are besieging Troy, the Trojan prince Troilus falls hopelessly in love with Criseyde, a Trojan maiden, and the two become lovers. They are separated, however, when her father, who has joined the enemy, arranges for her to be brought to the Greek camp. There, she is seduced by a Greek officer. When Troilus learns of her infidelity, he becomes enraged and charges into battle to confront the offending officer, but is tragically killed by the mighty Greek warrior Achilles. Chaucerian scholar D.S. Brewer sums up Chaucer's literary achievement in *Troilus*, saying that the work is

> rich in vivid realistic touches and convincing dialogue, yet learned and magnificent; noble, tender, and sympathetic, yet humorous, even with a touch of cynicism. Everywhere it is penetrated by Chaucer's compassionate and keen observation of the contradictions of earthly life that give rise both to humor and tragedy.

Chaucer's ability to capture the balance between life's comic and tragic elements would become even more apparent in *The Canterbury Tales*, which he began not long after finishing *Troilus*.

THE FORMATIVE IDEA FOR "SOME KIND OF COMEDY"

The period in which Chaucer produced *The Canterbury Tales*, the work considered most mature and least influenced by other writers, is often referred to as his English period, lasting from about 1386 until his death fourteen years later. Even while still working on *Troilus*, Chaucer toyed with the idea of writing a long work consisting of several short tales bound together in some thematic manner. To this end, early in 1386 he began working on *The Legend of Good Women*. His projected goal was to create an opening prologue that would introduce nineteen noble women from ancient history and mythology, including Cleopatra, Medea, and Thisbe, and follow this with a tale for each of the women. But he soon grew tired of what he apparently saw as too monotonous a literary scheme and abandoned the work before he had finished the eighth tale. Clearly he liked the idea of a collection of loosely related tales, but felt the need for a larger, more diversified, and more colorful literary palette from which to create.

Perhaps another factor that influenced Chaucer to put aside *Legend* was its overall serious tone. He longed to express himself in a lighter vein, as evidenced by a brief addenda that appears at the end of *Troilus* in which he suggests that he wishes to put tragedy to rest and asks God to "send yet to your maker, before he dies, the ability to compose in the manner of some kind of comedy." Scholars view this as a clear reference to his still formative idea for what became the Canterbury story collection.

Chaucer apparently began working on *The Canterbury Tales* late in 1386. Partly because the projected work was so long and wide in scope, and also because he faithfully kept up his duties as a civil servant, often leaving little time for writing, the task dragged on and on. He completed various groups of tales in three stages spanning a total of about fourteen years, also somehow finding the time to compose other, shorter works, such as the *Treatise on the Astrolabe,* finished in 1392 for his then ten-year-old son Lewis. But the massive Canterbury collection was still far from finished when Chaucer died in 1400 (the exact date is uncertain but traditionally accepted as October 25). His reputation as a poet was by that time so great that it almost completely overshadowed his accomplishments as a public servant and he was buried in London's Westminster Abbey, at the time a singular honor for a commoner. In succeeding generations, the famous Poet's Corner grew up around his tomb, a prestigious enclave featuring monuments to Spenser, Shakespeare, Milton, Dickens, Tennyson, and other English literary greats.

INTRODUCTION OF THE CAST OF CHARACTERS

The Canterbury Tales was incomplete at Chaucer's death, and no notes survive suggesting what further stories and characters he may have envisioned for the work. Likewise, no records indicate how he came up with the idea of making the storytellers pilgrims on a holy journey and whether any or all of these characters were based on real people the poet had met on an actual pilgrimage. Some scholars have suggested that Chaucer went on a pilgrimage to Canterbury in April 1387. At the time, his wife was ill (she died a few months later) and it was common practice to go on holy pilgrimage to pray for the recovery of an ailing loved one. Also, in the introduction to the *Man of Law's Tale* and its prologue, Chaucer mentions a specific date and time—April 18 at 10:00 A.M.—that might be a reference to the departure time of his real pilgrimage.

Regardless of whether it was based on the author's experiences on a real journey, the Canterbury pilgrimage proved a brilliant setting for the collection of comic/tragic tales Chaucer had in mind. As noted Chaucerian scholar and translator F.N. Robinson puts it, "The device of the pilgrimage is one of the happiest ever employed in a collection of stories. It afforded Chaucer an opportunity to bring together a representative group of various classes of society, united by a common religious purpose, yet not so dominated by that purpose as to be unable to give themselves over to enjoyment."

These diverse personalities are first introduced in the General Prologue to the *Tales*, in which the twenty-nine pilgrims gather at the Tabard Inn in Southwark, a suburb of London, in preparation for a holy trek to Canterbury, located some fifty miles to the southeast. The party includes a noble knight and his squire, a franklin (landowner), a rich merchant, a colorful middle-class widow known as the Wife of Bath, a doctor, a lawyer, a sailor, a low-class miller, and various other tradesmen, as well as diverse representatives of churches and convents, including a prioress, a parson, and several nuns and priests. Joining the group is Chaucer himself, that is, a somewhat fictionalized and at times unflattering version of his own character. The inn's host, Harry Bailly, proposes that the pilgrims pass the time while on the journey by engaging in a storytelling competition. Each member of the group will tell two stories on the way to Canterbury and two more on the return leg of the trip.

The General Prologue is ingenious, both as a way to introduce the cast of characters and as a device that provides a measure of structure and unity to the collection of tales that follows. The famous Chaucerian scholar Donald R. Howard comments in *Chaucer: His Life, His Works, His World:*

> The General Prologue is what makes *The Canterbury Tales* tick. It gives coherence to the whole, hovers over the arrangement of the tales and their assignment to appropriate tellers. The tales and tellers are uniquely a group in a complex dramatic relationship—a society in little—who gravitate toward each other on principles of class and group solidarity, or fall into competition because of traditional enmities or differences of temperament, age, and sex. Group dynamics direct their alliances and aggressions, which in turn direct the "plot" of the pilgrimage through debates on issues like marriage, parodies of others' tales, or personal animosity and revenge.... When people like [these] pilgrims hear or read a tale, each will find something different in it; they will see the characters with reference to their familiar worlds or their selves, and twist the plot to serve their fantasies.

THE FIRST STAGE OF THE WRITING

Chaucer wrote the General Prologue during the first phase of his production of the *Tales*, a period lasting from about 1386 to 1388. Phase one also saw the completion of the first pilgrim story, the *Knight's Tale*, which tells of the competition between two knights—cousins who are both equally strong, noble, and virtuous—for the hand of a highborn lady. The climax of the tale is a tournament in which one knight dies fighting for her; this leaves his cousin free to marry her and live happily ever after. Here, Chaucer went beyond the popular medieval chivalric romance, typically a story of love, adventure, and warrior derring-do, by introducing the element of unequal justice. That the knight who dies is as good and worthy as the one who lives seems inherently unfair and conjures up the concept of unsympathetic gods toying with the lives of human beings. Scholar Maurice Hussey explains:

> The story tells of destruction, of pain and misery brought upon human beings by gods concerned only with their own dignities. It concludes with a long philosophical speech by

Theseus, the lady's brother, in which he attempts to fit this destructive element into a pattern of divine order; and this speech is a magnificent embodiment of intellectual struggle, of the *difficulty* philosophy has in accounting for certain aspects of human life. These modifications of the basic romance vision turn the *Knight's Tale* into a work which at once expresses and transcends the essential qualities of medieval romance. It is one of the supreme achievements of courtly literature in the Middle Ages.

The tone of the remaining three tales Chaucer wrote during phase one contrasts markedly with that of the stately and philosophical *Knight's Tale*. These were his first three fabliaux, or short anecdotes featuring outlandish comic situations and/or rustic, bawdy humor. The fabliaux told by the Miller, Reeve (a manorial administrator), and Cook represent a new direction for Chaucer. First, instead of drawing his plots and characters from formal French, Latin, or Italian literary traditions, as he had done with *Troilus and Criseyde* and the *Knight's Tale*, he went directly to popular folktales and indecent jokes that had been handed down by word of mouth through the generations. This opened up a wealth of appealing comic ideas and situations to explore. Second, the fabliau idiom allowed Chaucer to utilize the coarse, unpolished words and phrases of everyday speech. This touch, along with his unwavering attention to descriptive detail, creates a remarkable air of realism in these tales. A perfect example is his description of the carpenter's house in the *Miller's Tale*, which includes such incredibly vivid details as a red cover on the cupboard in the student's room and a hole through which the cat used to crawl in and out.

Chaucer also endowed some of the realistic speech of his often lowbred fabliau characters with a quality then novel to formal writing. According to Donald Howard:

> In Phase One [of the writing of the *Tales*], Chaucer for the first time in English literature, perhaps in any literature, used dialect. He began the Reeve's Prologue having the Reeve speak in an approximation of East Anglian dialect [spoken in a region not far north of London]. We get enough of this to *imagine* he goes on speaking in dialect, though in fact he lapses into standard English. . . . Then Chaucer went a step further: while we may still imagine the Reeve's Tale being told in East Anglian, he has the two clerks speak a broad northern dialect, imitated with surprising accuracy. It appears that in this sequence of tales, which degenerate in their tone and morality, Chaucer wanted to show language itself degenerating, splitting apart into mutually incomprehensible varieties.

CHAUCER'S BATTLE OF THE SEXES

The second phase of the making of *The Canterbury Tales* spanned the years 1389 to 1396. In this period Chaucer wrote several new tales, including those of the Wife of Bath, Clerk, Merchant, Summoner, and Friar, and linked them together thematically by making them part of a larger extended discussion. The discussion concerns various aspects of the institution of marriage. The Wife, by virtue of having been married numerous times, purports to be a sort of resident expert on the subject and kicks off the discussion. First, in the prologue to her tale, she recalls anecdotes from her own life to make the point that the happiest marriages are those in which the wife is the boss. The following lines are typical of her tone:

> I shall speak truth, of the husbands I had,
> Three of them were good and two were bad.
>
> . . . .
> So help me God, I laugh when I remember
> How pitifully by night I made them work;
> And by my faith I set no store by it.
> They had given me their gold and their treasure;
> I had no need to make further effort
> To win their love, or pay them any respect.
>
> . . . .
> I governed them so well, according to my law,
> That each of them was very happy and eager
> To bring me gay things from the fair.
> They were most happy when I spoke fairly to them;
> For God knows, I nagged them spitefully.

She then elaborates on the same theme in her tale, which concerns one of King Arthur's knights who is condemned to die for raping a young maiden. At the last moment, the ladies of the court ask the king to give the knight another chance. His life should be spared, they suggest, if in the course of a year he can find the answer to the riddle: What do women most desire? With the help of an ugly old sorceress, he discovers the answer, namely that women most desire sovereignty over their husbands.

As the import of the Wife's prologue and tale seems to threaten the authority of all men, it provokes what can be described as a verbal battle of the sexes among several of the pilgrims. The Clerk, for example, tells a story set in what he sees as an ideal former age in which wives were very patient and submissive to their husbands. Long ago, he relates, a wealthy lord married a poor peasant girl and over the course of twenty years subjected her to a series of seemingly cruel tests of her patience and loyalty, including taking her children from her and pretending to have murdered them. She endured it all, repeatedly professing her love and submission to his authority. Finally convinced that she was worthy to be his wife, he revealed her grown children to her and began treating her with affection and respect. In a similar attempt to rebut the Wife of Bath's arguments, the Merchant first complains about his own unhappy marriage to an overbearing wife and then provides a tale about a deceitful young wife who cheats on and lies to her kindly, trusting husband.

The tales in this so-called Marriage Group, like those of the fabliaux in phase one of the writing of the *Tales*, illustrate how Chaucer derived several of his plots and characters from common folklore and then added his own twists, philosophical points, and rich description. In the case of the *Merchant's Tale*, for instance, F.N. Robinson explains that

> the kernel of the story is a popular *märchen* [folk story]. It is known to folklorists as the "Pear-Tree Episode," and is widely disseminated [distributed] in Europe and Asia. It serves the Merchant as an example of the wicked wiles of women. But the pear-tree story . . . is only a small part of the Merchant's discourse. Here, as in the case of Chaucer's [other tales in this phase], the simple plot is richly elaborated by description, comment, and characterization. . . . And the whole story is handled with great dramatic effect by the Merchant, himself unhappily mated, to give point to his bitter condemnation of matrimony and to the women to whose evil devices it exposes men.

DIFFERING VIEWS OF THE SAME TALE

As near as scholars can tell, during the last phase of the creation of the Canterbury collection, lasting from 1396 to his death in 1400, Chaucer penned the tales that lead up to the end of the host's storytelling game and the pilgrims' arrival at Canterbury cathedral. These include the stories of the Canon's Yeoman, Manciple, Parson, and Pardoner. Of these, the *Yeoman's Tale* is of particular interest, for it is perhaps, from the standpoint of the author's own feelings and life experiences, one of the most personal in the whole Canterbury collection. The content of the tale and its possible relationship to Chaucer's real life also illustrate how modern scholars often differ widely in interpreting the sources, meanings, and significance of his stories and characters.

In the prologue to the tale, a canon, loosely defined in medieval terms as a member of a respected religious order, and his yeoman, or servant, catch up to the pilgrim party after a mad gallop on horseback. The sociable Harry Bailly asks the Yeoman if his master would care to tell a tale. In trying to answer, the talkative servant begins to reveal how the Canon makes a living as a fraudulent alchemist, in prescientific times a person who claimed the ability to turn base metals into gold. The Canon becomes increasingly nervous and warns the Yeoman to be quiet; but the servant, who obviously holds his master in great contempt, continues the exposé until the flustered Canon, anticipating the pilgrims' ridicule, leaps back on his steed and rides away. After cursing the Canon and renouncing his allegiance to him, the Yeoman launches into a tirade about the tricks and phony devices used by alchemists to dupe people into thinking they will become rich. In small part, he says:

Seven years I've served this canon, but no more
Do I know about his science than before I met him.
All that I once had I have lost because of him;
And, God knows, so have many more men than me.
· · · · · · · · · · · · · ·
That slippery science has made me so bare
That I've no goods, wherever I may fare;
And I am still so deeply in debt as a result,
In truth, of the gold that I have borrowed,
That I'll never be able to repay it as long as I live.
Let every man heed my warning forever!

The Yeoman then tells a story about a canon (not his former master) who, upon encountering a priest who believes alchemy is true science, takes advantage of the unsuspecting man. Employing a common alchemist's trick, the canon stealthily enlists the priest's aid in changing copper into silver. To gain the holy man's confidence, the canon demonstrates the conversion; but of course, he accomplishes this not by magic, but by deft sleight of hand. Convinced, the priest begs for the formula and promptly pays forty pounds for it, supposedly a bargain price. The crooked canon then takes his leave, never to be seen again by the unfortunate priest.

Some scholars have suggested that the exposure of the falsity of alchemy in the *Yeoman's Tale* was Chaucer's indignant response to having been cheated himself by a canon-alchemist. A few who advance this hypothesis have even suggested that a specific canon, William Shuchirch of Windsor, who has been documented as having practiced alchemy, was the culprit who hoodwinked Chaucer. If true, this would explain the detailed and accurate accounts of the alchemist's art in the tale; presumably, once duped, Chaucer would have searched at every turn for information about how fraudulent alchemists operated.

On the other hand, many scholars feel that the evidence for this theory is weak and suggest that the tale simply illustrates Chaucer's extensive knowledge of his society and the characters, good and bad, who populated it. According to Robinson, episodes such as the one described by the Yeoman were probably "a matter of too common experience. They make a good story, and the Canon and his Yeoman, whether or not drawn from life, are among the most lifelike of Chaucer's characters."

A REMARKABLE PICTURE OF LIFE'S DIVERSITY

Considering *The Canterbury Tales* as a whole, incidents and characters drawn from real life, like those in the *Yeoman's Tale*, abound throughout the work. And yet, as discussed earlier, Chaucer also ingeniously integrated stories from folklore, famous characters and myths from Greece and other ancient lands, and literary tales from medieval France and Italy. The Doctor, for example, says that his tale is taken from the famous history book of the ancient Roman writer Livy; the tales of the Franklin and Monk are reworkings of pieces from the *Decameron* story collection of Chaucer's older contemporary, the renowned Italian poet Giovanni Boccaccio; the Clerk tells a story first set down by Petrarch, the respected fourteenth-century Italian writer; the *Squire's Tale* comes from faraway central Asia, then referred to as the Orient; the basic material for the *Second Nun's Tale* is found in holy Christian legend; the writings of the Roman poet Ovid are the source for the *Manciple's Tale*; and the fabliaux tales, such as those of the Reeve and Cook, though set in the English countryside, are styled on French originals.

It is a testament to Chaucer's imagination and writing skill that he was able to combine these many and diverse foreign styles, characters, and ideas, along with characters and ideas from his own experiences or of his own invention, into so harmonious a whole. Counting both the pilgrims and the people described in their tales, the work features literally hundreds of characters from dozens of societies and from all walks of life. And yet Chaucer smoothly integrates all of them, regardless of their original sources, into a single and masterful framework. Never does the reader doubt the authenticity of any of the pilgrims who make the journey through fourteenth-century southern England; nor do we doubt for a moment that such pilgrims would tell such tales. In a very real sense, their great diversity of types, backgrounds, and opinions is sorted and filtered through the viewpoint of the overall narrator, Chaucer himself. Thus, the *Tales* represents one man's personal vision of the diversity of life in his day. As Howard puts it, Chaucer's skillful blending of characters and ideas

> [gives] *The Canterbury Tales* the unique character of a hall with many mirrors set not facing each other in infinite reflection but at various angles, so that we see each component of the picture reflected in multiple views from different vantage points, see the wide-eyed narrator seeing it all, glimpse beneath his mask sometimes the role-playing author, and find ourselves in the picture trying to see it clearly.

The remarkable picture of life that Chaucer painted in words in *The Canterbury Tales* is even more indebted to his ability to observe the details of people's appearances and characters. For he captured not only the diversity of life, but also its reality. Indeed, says Hussey, "Chaucer is famous as the great poet of human reality, the one writer of so long ago in whose characters we can recognize our own neighbors." Ironically, in the General Prologue the pilgrim named Chaucer apologizes for his shortcomings as a descriptive narrator. Preparing to introduce the characters, he says:

> I think it appropriate
> To tell you about the nature
> Of each of them, as they appeared to me,
> And who they were, and of what station in life.

And a while later he adds:

> But first I beg you, out of your courtesy,
> That you ascribe it not to my crudeness,
> Even though I speak plainly in this narration,
> To tell you their words and behavior.

This was only the overly modest Chaucer-the-character speaking, of course. Millions of enchanted and thoroughly satisfied readers over the centuries can vouch that the real Chaucer was anything but crude and plain and had not the slightest reason to apologize.

CHAPTER 1

The Structure and Language of *The Canterbury Tales*

READINGS ON
THE CANTERBURY TALES

Where Did Chaucer Get His Idea for *The Canterbury Tales*?

Donald R. Howard

For centuries, scholars have argued about the nature and source of Chaucer's initial idea for the form and structure of *The Canterbury Tales*. In this essay, Donald Howard, former professor of English at Stratford University and one of the foremost Chaucer experts of the twentieth century, proposes that a poetic idea initially comes out of an author's everyday life experiences, especially from what he or she hears from others. Much of what the author knows about the world, in fact, comes from these rumors, or "tidings." But because any author's personal experiences are limited and rumors are often unreliable, the idea he or she conceives is usually abstract and difficult to define until it is actually written down. Then, regardless of whether it was based on true or false rumors, on the printed page the idea suddenly takes on a quality of truth all its own. Thus, a work like *The Canterbury Tales*, though essentially fiction, contains a strong element of truth in that it conveys the author's true feelings and beliefs about people and the world as well as reflects or evokes the reader's feelings and beliefs. It is a small mirror of what life and the world are like at the time of the telling.

Every literary work was once an idea in its author's mind: when we read the work we grasp the idea at least in part, and whatever formal qualities we find in the work—unity or form or structure—could not exist without that idea. If we can suppose this, what can we suppose about the idea of *The Canterbury Tales*? Until recently most critics have supposed that Chaucer's idea of *The Canterbury Tales* was a simple

From Donald R. Howard, "Chaucer's Idea of an Idea," *Essays & Studies*, vol. 29 (1976), pp. 39-55. Reprinted by permission of the publisher, The English Association.

one: they have said that the work is at base a realistic description of a four-day journey to Canterbury, that if the author had lived longer he would have added more tales, described overnight stops and the journey home, that the heart or backbone of the work is the tales themselves (especially the bawdy ones), and that in these his great achievement was in breaking with convention and going direct to life. In reaction to this estimate of *The Canterbury Tales* a more recent trend in Chaucer criticism has advanced an even simpler idea: that the pilgrimage to Canterbury is a metaphor for the pilgrimage of human life, that the pilgrimage as a penitential act is the heart or backbone of the work (or the 'fruit'), and that the tales are therefore 'chaff'—which, however, I am happy to add, no amount of wind has managed to blow away.

All these opinions assume that *The Canterbury Tales* has a single controlling idea behind it, one that we can articulate and see executed in the work. If we politely suppose that each is correct . . . 'in some degree', then taken together they are 'the' idea of *The Canterbury Tales*. And this means that the idea is not a simple one at all but ornate, many-faceted, labyrinthine—may I say Gothic—in its complexity. Nevertheless, it is *an* idea which existed in *a* poet's mind and is embodied in *a* work. It is composed of many characteristic ideas of his period; but taken together it is singular, unique—may I say Chaucerian—in its individual embodiment. . . .

In my book *The Idea of the Canterbury Tales* . . . I have claimed to have seen inside the mind of Geoffrey Chaucer and to have described the idea which existed in his mind, which moved him to write *The Canterbury Tales*, which informed its whole and its parts, which is embodied in it and makes it live—an outrageous claim, the daughter of Megalomania [egotism] and Obsession, as it must seem—but I insist that it is less outrageous than previous claims. When a critic says that Chaucer meant to write over a hundred tales which he never wrote (because one ebullient character proposes that the others tell that many tales), or when a critic says that Chaucer meant to describe a journey home which he never described, in a kind of description no medieval author had written, they have made claims far more outrageous. They have claimed to know a startling, original plan which he had in mind but failed to accomplish. I claim to observe a plan sufficiently characteristic of his age which he had in mind and largely did accomplish.

ART IMITATES LIFE

To my claim there is still an objection which can be raised. The objector might say, 'You are presupposing an idea which existed in the author's mind and informs his work, but isn't this *idea* of an idea a modern one . . . the sort of superstition we hold when we praise a modern book for "tightness" or demote it for "sprawl" or "self-indulgence"?' But my reply is no. The kind of idea I have in mind is a medieval conception, one which was part of medieval aesthetics and rhetoric. . . . The Middle Ages, though it adopted on the whole a mimetic theory of art [advocating that art imitates or mimics], held that the object of that mimesis was not 'nature' but the interior reality which exists in the artist's mind. The painter does not paint a rose; he paints his idea of the rose, and this idea or 'quasi-idea' is of a higher order than any single physical specimen and anterior to any artistic embodiment. Edgar De Bruyne in *The Esthetics of the Middle Ages* describes the doctrine when he writes, 'The material work of art is not necessarily a faithful copy of the visible form (a roof is not a reproduction of a mountain range), but it is inevitably a representation of what the artist conceives in his soul. The form is above all an imitation of this spiritual model'. . . .

Such an idea of an idea was present in the rhetorical writings of the Middle Ages and was thus part of the medieval conception of poetical composition. The emphasis was on the experience of the writer rather than of the reader, on the *making* of the poetical work. The best-known expression of the idea is in the opening lines of Geoffrey of Vinsauf's *Poetria Nova:* 'If a man has a house to build, his impetuous hand does not rush into action. The measuring line of his mind first lays out the work, and he mentally outlines the successive steps in a definite order. The mind's hand shapes the entire house before the body's hand builds it. Its mode of being is archetypal [ideal in form] before it is actual.' We know Chaucer was familiar with this passage because he translated it in the *Troilus*, assigning it to Pandarus as a thought which occurs to him as he plans to arrange the love affair.

About this medieval conception of a poetical idea there is a question which I side-stepped in *The Idea of the Canterbury Tales* and would like to consider in what follows. If we can fairly assume that Chaucer's idea of a poem squared with the medieval conception, did his understanding of that conception, his personal grasp of it and his private thoughts about it, have an idiosyncratic or individual character? Did his idea of a literary idea in some ways verge from the traditional one which he might have had from Dante or Geoffrey of Vinsauf? I say it did. And it differed in a way which scattered seed throughout the history of English letters. Ezra Pound [well-known twentieth-century American poet] said that 'no-one will ever gauge or measure English poetry until they know how much of it, how full a gamut of its qualities, is already *there on the page* of Chaucer'. I say that Chaucer's idea of an idea is what at base explains the important place he holds in English literary tradition. . . .

TIDINGS FROM THE HOUSE OF RUMOR

While his predecessors likened the process of making a poem to that of building a house, Chaucer . . . represented the realm of poetry as itself a house. And he imagined another kind of house from which we get poems, the House of Rumor [the unseen place whence comes various rumors, or tidings, about people and the world]. . . . Daedalus, the mythical builder of the labyrinth [a huge, mazelike structure described in ancient Greek mythology], was the architect or builder *par excellence.* And the labyrinth he created, that mythic house, was in the Middle Ages itself a symbol of building. In churches and Gothic cathedrals especially in Italy and France we find a labyrinth or maze inlaid as a mosaic on a wall or pavement. In some cases the architect of a Gothic cathedral inscribed his name in the centre of the labyrinth which stood at the centre of the cathedral floor: the builder symbolized God the creator and the labyrinth symbolized creation. It is widely believed, but not proved, that the pavement labyrinths of Gothic cathedrals were used as substitute pilgrimages—the penitent crawled on his knees along the unicursal way from the entrance of the labyrinth to its centre, which was called *ciel* or *Jérusalem*; in France pavement labyrinths were called *Dédales* or *chemins de Jérusalem.* So while the labyrinth symbolized the created universe, it also symbolized the pilgrimage of human life, the world. In appropriating the figure of the labyrinth to describe the House of Rumor, Chaucer seems to have suggested that the source of poems, this interior or mentalistic realm, is the world itself, whose end is to be subsumed in the timeless universe. A poetical idea ultimately comes out of a remembered or reported experience *of the world*; its meaning is complete only at the end of time, when the world is complete. Poems are by their very nature among the transitory things of this world.

This 'House of Rumor' which is like the labyrinth turns out to be a giant wicker cage whirling about, which both holds and filters tidings. The centrality of tidings in this conception of poetry explains why the House of Rumor has the final and climactic position. These tidings are passed about by word of mouth, they become bloated and distorted in the telling, and some escape through the doors or cracks of the House of Rumor. It might be said that they are to poems what phonemes are to words or morphemes to sentences. So if we want to know Chaucer's idea of a poetical idea we have to know what he meant by tidings. According to the OED [*Oxford English Dictionary*] a tiding is something that has happened, an event—and more often the announcement of such an event, in other words a piece of news. In Chaucer it seems to mean the announcement of such news by word of mouth or by letter. Tidings don't bear a one-to-one relation to the events they report—you can have more than one tiding for one event, and you can have a tiding for a non-event: Chaucer twice . . . makes it indisputably clear that a tiding is a tiding whether it is true or false. Thus he finds in the House of Rumor the most notorious kinds of liars. . . .

In this Chaucer was taking a radical position. Where medieval rhetoric held that poetry, or the idea of a poem, originates in the interior world of ideas, he held that poetry has its origin in rumor, in spoken language. In Chaucer's uses of the term a tiding can 'befall' or 'come' but otherwise it is something you 'say', 'tell', or (most often) 'hear'. Behind it is something that happened or is said to have happened. Tidings never come from reading: if you are a poet and you are looking for tidings, you put aside your book, as indeed Chaucer does in all his dream-visions. But from the book he goes direct to fantasy, not 'life'; the chitchat he hears can even come from talking birds. In pointing to the basic relation of poetry to the spoken language Chaucer seems to have had in mind not the stream of speech as it exists in objective reality but the stream of speech as it exists in our thoughts. . . .

TRUTH IS RELATIVE

What this must mean is that poets rise or fall, live or die, on the sheer grounds of whether anyone is reading them and talking about them. The fate of a poem depends on its readers, and on different *kinds* of readers. Chaucer acknowledges this in *The Canterbury Tales* when he makes the famous reference to turning over the leaf and choosing another tale. . . . Each of the tales told on the Canterbury pilgrimage is from this point of view a tiding—a bit of *lore*—heard and reported by a pilgrim for those pilgrims who share common attitudes and values with him; and then all the tales are 'rehearsed' in sequences by the narrator for various readerships or for a readership with a taste for various kinds of tales.

Now it is just in these sequences of tidings, re-told by the narrator and re-heard by us, that we see embodied in *The Canterbury Tales* what was foreshadowed in *The House of Fame* [an earlier work of Chaucer's in which he suggests that speech is made up of tidings, some of them true, others false, and all of them abstract and difficult to define]. The objective truth of a tiding is of no consequence; when it is reified in a tale or a poem or a book it becomes a *thing*, or part of a thing—and 'thing' was a Middle English word for 'poem'—that exists in the world for a certain time. As part of such a thing, every tiding is true in one way or another. You have to *look* for the truth of a tiding, and not all tidings are true in the same way, but every tiding is authentic. . . . It tells us something but the burden is on us to know what that something is. St Augustine said that if you have an image of a man in a mirror it cannot be a true image without being a false man. And he went on to ask, 'if the fact that they are false in one respect helps certain things to be true in another respect, why do we fear falseness so much and seek truth as such a great good? . . . Will we not admit that these things make up truth itself, that truth is so to speak put together from them?'

In *The Canterbury Tales* Chaucer took this position about the relative truth of fictions. And he made his position clear by setting up the Parson as a foil. The Parson in his Prologue isn't smart enough to see what Chaucer saw. . . . He takes the position of naïve realism—he thinks all fables are lies and all lies are bad. . . . Chaucer's idea was the reverse. If you tell a tale, true or false, your choice of the tale and your motive and manner in telling it tells a truth about you. There is a truth somewhere, but it is relative, various—and partial. Chaucer never claims to possess the *whole* truth. . . . He quotes St Paul that all that is written is written for our doctrine and says 'that is my intent'. The question that remains is of course how we *get* the doctrine out of all that is written. And Chaucer's answer, very unlike the Parson's but not unlike St Paul's, is that it is up to us to find it in our own way. We use the foolish things of the world to confound the wise. Part of Chaucer's idea is simply that no literary idea can approach its full potential of 'poetic truth' unless it engages the reader's interest and enlists his participation. It demands of us an act of will, for the truth of a poem is in *our* idea of it.

EVERYTHING IS ONLY AS IT SEEMS

Now it is undeniable that one way of gaining the truth from a poem was to read it allegorically. This was to an extent true of medieval notions about reading; it was much truer after Chaucer's time and well into the seventeenth century that poems, especially pagan poems, were understood to be 'mysteriously meant'. . . . But there was another notion about poetic truth, in some ways harder for us to grasp because it is more familiar to us—because it has never died and because we take it for granted. And this was Chaucer's idea. But it is not an idea in the usual sense—not something he thought consciously but something he *did*. It was what we would call a feeling: Chaucer seems to have had a feeling that at the heart of any literary work is something that has happened, or at least been told, a 'tiding'. True or false, some tidings catch our fancy and some do not—who knows why? Chaucer followed his instincts and acted on this feeling. We might compare the way most of us would describe our 'idea' of how to teach a class or write a paper: we do what works for us, and what works for us *is* our idea even though often enough we cannot state that idea except by inventing examples or telling anecdotes. I am claiming then that at the heart of Chaucer's idea was a feeling of which he was not perhaps fully conscious but which *I* am able to articulate—a most outrageous claim, as it may seem, the very daughter of Fatuity and Delusion—but I am not alone in thinking it. On the contrary, I am indebted to that scholar who has dealt most penetratingly with Chaucer's use of medieval rhetoric, Robert Payne. As Payne has recently reminded us, Chaucer

knew that no artist can provide what he thinks are the necessary and adequate aims for poetry unless he thinks he
knows what he is doing. But, Payne adds, Chaucer also knew
'that for even the best of men, what one thinks he is doing is
never quite exactly what he is doing'.

Then if the heart of Chaucer's idea was in what he did
more than in what he thought, what did he do? It used to be
said that what he did was to break with convention and go
direct to life; now, for a generation, scholars have been toil-
ing to prove that he broke with life and went direct to convention. This counter-trend has produced a sort of universal
rule of thumb that nothing in Chaucer is what it seems. . . . If
this had been so, how could we explain the enthusiasm of
readers in the centuries after Chaucer's death for Chaucer's
pilgrims and tales, much the same pilgrims and tales we feel
enthusiasm for—the Pardoner, who attracted the anony-
mous author of the *Tale of Beryn*, or the Wife's tale, which attracted John Milton as a study of 'the discommodities of
marriage', as he called it, or the Squire's tale, which attracted
Spenser and Milton? Their enthusiasm argues powerfully in
favour of Chaucer's idea, whose universal rule of thumb was
that everything is *exactly and only what it seems*, that every
utterance is *exactly and only what it says*. The Pardoner is
only the Pardoner; Chauntecleer, Chauntecleer; Pandarus,
Pandarus; the Wife, the Wife. We must practise a rule of ab-
stinence, must do as the Nun's Priest counsels—keep our
eyes open and our mouths shut. Chaucer seems to have believed that you can get tidings, can 'tell a tale after a man',
can 'rehearse' it in such a way that people will react as Harry
Bailly and the pilgrims react, by laughing, by being dumb-
founded, by arguing, by calling a halt, by telling another tale.
What causes this reaction is the uniqueness and . . . the authenticity, of each personage and utterance. This authenticity is what *we* perceive as Chaucer's irony: Chaucer teases
us—or we tease ourselves—into supposing that things are
something bigger and the characters something more than
what they seem, and the irony is that they are not. They are
always and only themselves; it is for us to make of them
what we will. . . .

IN THE END: SILENCE

Seen from this point of view, the Wife is an ironic figure because she . . . is always and only the Wife. We do not under-

stand her. She does not understand herself. Chaucer does not understand her and does not claim to. When he says she had five husbands . . . the irony is that he means exactly and only that. . . . It is a tiding; we may make of it what we can. And perhaps the best we can make of it is that our actual experience of the world is precisely of this kind. If you met the Wife, wouldn't you wonder what she'd been like before that first marriage? Isn't it just that fomenting time of her life which she would not tell you anything about—would probably not fully understand herself, or remember? And isn't one explanation of her complicated marital history the possibility that in her formative youth she *was* without company? What we don't know is what is interesting and important here. The phrase is pregnant with meaning but the only scholarly way to decide that meaning is to follow the OED and create an intermediate category—which is to call it ambiguous. We perceive such ambiguities as ironic, but the irony is *in us*—it is in our response to Chaucer's idea, which was to express accurately those tidings which experience and the world presented to him. If you call it deadpan or tongue-in-cheek or ironic you are only acknowledging, what is surely true, that Chaucer knew he could count on this 'ironic' response in us, or most of us. Irony is an acquired taste, and not everyone acquires it. So Chaucer's idea was risky and theatrical, 'distanced', and highly disciplined. It calls upon a frame of mind in us—anticipates that frame of mind and in part inculcates it [instills it in our minds]. It is not a 'strategy', for strategy by definition manipulates. It is rather a stance which invites and permits.

It was this part of his idea, this stance, which Chaucer bequeathed to English literature. It has been the mainstay of English fiction, the essence of the drama and the novel as they were to develop. The artist effaces or disguises himself, throws attention on the 'realities' of his story, the 'true history' he purports to relate. But the authenticity he offers is not in realities or history or even in tidings. It is in appearances, in the way things *seem*. It is therefore a wholly mentalistic or psychological phenomenon: the tiding reported by the writer and acknowledged by the reader can be true or false. It has its authenticity in inner experience—in the mentalistic world of Rumor and Fame. Fiction in this tradition deflects our attention to *seeming*: to the author's or narrator's mind, or to one character's mind, and always in some measure to the reader's mind. Its verisimilitude resides not in details but in the aura of the unknown and unknowable that pervades details and is the essence of 'tidings'. . . .

But there is another side to Chaucer's idea of an idea which makes his abstemious way of putting tidings on paper altogether compatible with medieval thought: he acknowledged that it was all *only an idea.* In the last analysis tidings are noise, and while we may grasp a truth from the total experience of hearing or reading them, from the experience of contemplating *seeming,* the better way is silence. For this reason Chaucer always rejects in the end the very thing he is in search of. . . . At the end of *The Canterbury Tales,* before the Parson's loquacious discourse, in the Manciple's tale, the talking crow is deprived of his ability to 'countrefete the speche of every man . . . whan he sholde telle a tale', Phebus the god of poetry destroys his harp, and the audience is bombarded with a collection of proverbs on the virtue of silence. Chaucer's idea of a literary idea included the recognition that a work of literature is only one of many things in this world, that it lives in an inner world of ideas and sententiae [brief observations of and comments on life] and memories which alone give duration and authenticity to tidings, and that this inner world too will vanish in the end.

Chaucer's Use of a Game as the Inner Framework for the *Tales*

Glending Olson

Having his characters play a storytelling game at the suggestion of the Host, Harry Bailly, is one of the ways that Chaucer tied the diverse stories of *The Canterbury Tales* together. Like other literary figures of his era, Chaucer tried to conform to the basic literary principle of a unified structure set down many centuries before by the Greek philosopher Aristotle, whose influence on the culture of the Late Middle Ages was profound. But the highly inventive Chaucer was not content merely to set up the game and have every character play it the same way. In this selection from *The Idea of Medieval Literature*, Glending Olson, professor of English at Cleveland State University, explains how Chaucer cleverly developed and altered the concept of the game as the work progressed. According to Olson, the game begins in an air of fun and good-natured interplay, but eventually it degenerates into a more strained atmosphere in which insults are exchanged and one character calls for the game to end.

The *Canterbury Tales* is a collection of narratives bound together in a frame that has two central features—a pilgrimage and a game. The pilgrimage is the outer framing device, the occasion for the gathering together of the company of storytellers; the game is a second, inner, framing device, the organizing principle that brings the stories into being. Chaucer did not have to have his pilgrims play a game in order to have them tell stories. Their prologues and tales could have emerged as part of conversation or debate or advice. . . . But he took the option [his Italian contemporary

From *The Idea of Medieval Literature: New Essays on Chaucer and Medieval Culture in Honor of Donald R. Howard*, edited by James M. Dean and Christian K. Zacher (Newark, DE: University of Delaware Press, 1992). Copyright ©1992 by Associated University Presses, Inc. Reprinted with permission.

Giovanni] Boccaccio took in the *Decameron*—he made the storytelling the playing of a game. And we need to think about the implications of that choice. . . .

When Harry Bailly proposes, and the pilgrims accept, the playing of a game in order to provide comfort and mirth, the *Canterbury Tales* draws on a medieval understanding of the legitimacy and benefits of recreational play. . . . Here I want to explore in . . . detail one aspect of that understanding and its relevance to Chaucer's collection. For the beginning of the *Canterbury Tales*, what we call Fragment I, is a sequence of storytelling that parallels directly a sequence of thoughts about play and players that was commonplace in the later Middle Ages. Chaucer's idea of the Canterbury game, though it ends in something very different, begins as an enactment of some Aristotelian distinctions [those relating to the ancient Greek philosopher Aristotle].

THE MEDIEVAL CONCEPT OF PLAY

The *Nicomachean Ethics* [of Aristotle] discusses a number of virtues, one of which is a virtue in regard to play or entertainment . . . which was standard for the later Middle Ages. Chaucer . . . knew the principle by which Aristotle defined his virtues and their corresponding vices. . . . Aristotle treats the virtues as means between extremes, one of excess, one of defect. Courage, for example, is the virtue in regard to fear—the mean between cowardice, excessive fear, and recklessness, the lack of fear even in situations where it would be appropriate. Liberality, the virtue in regard to the use of wealth, is the mean between the excess of prodigality and the defect of avarice, both of which sins [the thirteenth-century Italian poet] Dante punishes in the fourth circle of *Inferno* and mentions again . . . in *Purgatorio* XXII. The mean in regard to play is *eutrapelia*, the excess *bomolochia*, the defect *agroica*—"wittiness," "buffoonerey," and "boorishness" are the usual modern English translations. . . .

The person who errs by excessive play is a *bomolochus* or buffoon. . . . Many medieval commentators stress that the excess of the buffoon lies not just in the quantity of his playing, in his failure to observe the necessary subordination of entertainment to seriousness, but also in the nature of his play, particularly the use of foul language. [Fourteenth-century French bishop and Aristotelian scholar] Nicole Oresme's French translation of the [*Nichomachean*] *Ethics* gives an interesting contemporary example of such excess. In his discussion of proper and improper language in play Aristotle had alluded briefly to old and new Greek comedy, contrasting the greater obscenity of the former with the more refined innuendo of the latter. His meaning was not totally clear to medieval commentators, but most recognized a moral judgment being made in regard to the decency of language in some kind of performance or composition. In a gloss on this passage Oresme explains that Aristotle's use of the term "comedies" refers to "plays such as those where one person represents St. Paul, another Judas, another a hermit," and that such plays sometimes include vulgar language, improper and distasteful. I take Oresme's present tense here to encompass contemporary [that is, fourteenth-century] as well as classical [ancient Greek] habits; his explication is telling not just for what it says about religious drama in his day but for [showing] ... the discussion of play in *Nicomachean Ethics* to have been a central point of reference for making judgments about forms of public entertainment, some of which we now call literature. . . .

THE KNIGHT, THE MILLER, AND THE REEVE

The treatment of play I have been delineating is certainly not the only medieval thinking on the subject. But it is, I believe, the dominant learned *secular* tradition, and its very secularity is perhaps as significant for understanding its importance to the *Canterbury Tales* as are the more detailed parallels I discuss shortly. The fact is that most medieval thinking about play (granting the bias of the surviving texts) is fundamentally moral rather than psychological or anthropological. That does not mean that such thinking need always be intended moralistically, or that it does not include insights into play compatible with other approaches; but it does suggest the likelihood that medieval reflections on play would at least work out of a conceptual framework that concerns itself less with the nature of play than with its ethical or social propriety. In this regard Aristotle's mean and extremes fit compatibly with medieval *distinctiones* on play based on biblical usage, which generally recognized that some playing was spiritual, some was evil or diabolical, and some more neutrally human or recreational. . . .

The Canterbury storytelling begins as a game to provide "comfort" and "mirthe." That fact alone serves to establish an initial secular delimitation, though one with its own claims to integrity. And despite the drama of spontaneity— the Knight wins by luck, the Miller interrupts, the Reeve takes offense at the Miller's story—an ordering principle appears among the first three tales, which reveal three distinct responses to the game that correspond to the Aristotelian analysis of the mean and the extremes in playing.

Particularly when read retrospectively, the portraits in the General Prologue suggest a triangulation of Knight-Miller-Reeve in regard to their social speech. The Knight [is] described first. . . .

The Knight is first of all a good man who has agreed to play a game, and he honors that agreement. The logic of his thinking in lines 853–54 merits notice: his welcoming of the cut follows upon his selection as the one to play first. I think the most probable interpretation of these lines is that the Knight is not necessarily eager to tell the first story, but having won the cut he *then* conducts himself in a manner suitable to the sense of "disport" that is appropriate to the purposes of the game. He has agreed to play, has found himself scheduled to lead off, and thus speaks according to the proper demands of recreational play. . . . His geniality is in fact an aspect of his moral goodness, the observation of the mean in regard to the social play that the company has committed itself to. And as we know, the Knight continues to support the game and its recreational goals subsequently— in his reconciliation of Pardoner and Host and in his cutting off of the Monk's depressing tragedies. He is as loyal in the company's play as in his lords' wars. . . .

Even Harry Bailly [the Host, who suggested the game in the first place], whose literary tastes are hardly aristocratic, appreciates . . . the Knight's Tale. . . . He turns to the Monk but gets instead the Miller, the drunken buffoon who has seen his chance to turn the ideals of the first story into laughter. The tone of the Miller's Tale is one of cheerful ridicule. . . . The tale mocks everyone, all for the sake of laughter. The Miller also derides himself and his wife. . . .

Following upon the Knight's noble entertainment and the Miller's churlish frivolity comes the Reeve's vicious retaliation. He is unable to let pass the swipe at carpenters that is merely a portion of the Miller's repertoire. . . . The Reeve is a sermonizer, deadly serious about everything; amusement has not mellowed him, nor humor moderated his infinite acerbity. He really is not capable of play, and his tale is so obviously an attack upon the Miller that it seems outside the spirit of the game. . . .

THE COOK AND THE HOST "HAVE WORDS"

Chaucer's exploration of how people play [does not] end with the Reeve's Tale. Both the Cook's Prologue and his fragmentary story deal principally with questions of play and truth in a way that is intellectually related to the game structure of the first fragment. . . .

When the Cook proposes to continue the storytelling game . . . it is quite clear that he wishes to continue in the same vein as the two previous speakers. . . . At this point, though, his speech appears no more degenerate or unrefined than the Miller's or Reeve's, and in fact his request to tell the next tale is rather more polite and respectful of the rules of the game. . . . It is the Host who surprises us, by telling the Cook that his tale needs to be good because his cuisine hasn't been. After sundry claims about the culinary and sanitary defects of the Cook's operation, Harry Bailly ends his gibing as abruptly as he started. . . .

At this point Harry Bailly becomes, perhaps, a *derisor*, a mocker, who . . . under cover of play seeks to embarrass someone else; because of the privileged status of speech made in play, his victims will not actually lose their reputation (a fact the mocker understands), but they will fear such a loss since the charges have been made public and could well be reasserted outside the special context of "game" which allows them to be at once both entertained and dismissed.

Or perhaps the Host's intentions remain purely playful, and his insults meant solely for amusement. Even if this were the case, he has approached the boundary at which it becomes difficult to know whether his raillery aims at *contemptus* [contempt] or *ludus* [play], and the Cook's response is intended to alert Harry Bailly that he is in danger of stepping over into territory where claims of play can no longer provide moral protection. . . .

The Cook's Prologue, then, tells us as much about the Host as about the Cook, and while there is no developed equation of either character with any traditional type of player of games, the issue raised in the exchange is a logical extension of the game given medieval thinking about playful speech. We have seen the mean and the extremes in regard to play, and now Chaucer brings to the fore one important aspect of excessive play not yet considered, the problem of drawing the line between game and earnest when playful language impugns someone else. The exchange occurs in a prologue that promises the telling of a "jape" in an atmosphere of "joye" and coarse hilarity, which is Chaucer's dramatic equivalent of the commentary treatment of mockery in the context of excessive play, whose chief representative in the first fragment is the Miller. The Miller has insulted the Reeve only as part of a desire to reduce everything to laughter. The Host's more pointed attack on the Cook claims similar status as "game and pley" yet is of a different order; it is what scholastic commentators, I think, would have defined as *derisio* [mockery] rather than *bomolochia* [buffoonery]. . . .

THE GAME DEGENERATES

The appearance of the Cook at the end of the first fragment . . . follows logically upon the previous sequence of tale-telling if we see it in light of medieval discussions of the morality of play: after presenting the mean and the extremes, Chaucer takes up the question of distinguishing between excessive play and mockery . . . [and] introduces us to a range of attitudes toward the game that will become ever more complicated as the *Canterbury Tales* progresses. In this regard the Cook's Prologue and Tale in particular point toward some of the most problematic and fascinating of the Canterbury performances, as some of Chaucer's richest characters, notably the Wife and the Pardoner, force us to look very closely at the ways in which their playing and their truthtelling are related.

Throughout the *Tales* the game is usually the norm. In places Chaucer reminds us, in one way or another, that beyond the game lies the pilgrimage—perhaps most obviously in the Pardoner's performance and exchange with the Host, where the breakdown of social agreeableness occurs in a context of phony promises of what should be a goal of the pilgrimage itself, spiritual absolution. But such episodes are the exception rather than the rule, though perhaps all the more telling for their infrequency; for the most part the linking passages are filled with the language of game and obligation, and with Harry Bailly's energetic and often overbearing presence as director of entertainment. But toward the end of the work ... something happens to the game. At its fullest this development encompasses the last three fragments. I want to mention, rather briefly, some aspects of Fragment IX only, which present a deliberately disturbing recapitulation [repetition] of some of the central features of the framing action in Fragment I. Part of Chaucer's idea of the Canterbury game is its degeneration; the Manciple's Prologue enacts such debasement of social conviviality [merriment] and playful speech as to make us uneasy with the game as a sufficient ordering principle, and correspondingly his tale ends in admonitions not to tell stories of any sort.

DRUNKENNESS AND LOSS OF DECORUM

The contrasts with the first fragment are quite specific. Although drunkenness appears throughout the pilgrimage and tales, drunkenness as it relates to storytelling is foregrounded most extensively in Fragments I and IX. The Miller's interruption is clearly due in part to his inebriation, yet whatever loss of control and decorum it implies in his case, he at least remains articulate, a participant in the game. The Cook's drunkenness in Fragment IX results in silence, sleep, nonparticipation. It is a more extreme version of the loss of reason that inebriation causes. Both Miller and Cook are "pale" because of drink, but the physical symptoms in the Cook's case are developed further to include glazed eyes and foul breath. A single line informs us that the Miller can scarcely keep his balance on horseback....

Whatever the reasons for the incompleteness of his tale at the start of the game, whatever the order in which Chaucer actually composed the scenes, the contrast between the Cook of Fragment I and the Cook of Fragment IX is striking and indicative of the substantially different view of Canterbury conviviality in the later fragments. The Cook now becomes the featured non-speaker among the pilgrims, excused by the Host from participation in the game on the grounds of inebriation. His fall from his horse is the most potent image in the Manciple's Prologue of the social behavior of the company having gone awry. In the muck lies ... a Canterbury pilgrim. Images of death, judgment, and hell flicker throughout the Prologue—the thief who might come upon the Cook, the association of his open mouth with hell-mouth. Whereas the Miller's drunkenness leads to a story that prompts laughter, the Cook's leads only to . . . reminders of mortality. . . .

THE PARSON REJECTS THE GAME

In the first fragment the Cook had warned the Host about the dangers of play that comes too close to the truth and in so doing had exposed a problem in the social uses of language well known to medieval commentators and moralists. In the ninth fragment too the Cook is a victim of insult, but here with no such teasing ambiguity as in his exchange with Harry Bailly. The Manciple "openly," to use the Host's own terminology, reproves the Cook for his drunkenness and hurls the kind of invective at him that . . . the Parson condemns as fostering disaccord and anger. Only when the Host reminds the Manciple that the Cook might similarly defame him does he reverse himself . . . and offer more wine to the Cook to placate him. What in the first fragment is a comic but subtle exploration of the problem of determining a borderline between play and insult, in which Harry self-consciously advertises his mockery as play, becomes in the ninth an instance of insult that, only in response to someone else's warning, attempts cynically and transparently to cover itself as jest. The secular norms of play no longer function as a governing communal standard but appear now as merely a convenient excuse for verbal attack, a self-interested afterthought. . . .

[Chaucer's] idea of the Canterbury game is an image of social and secular conviviality that establishes itself as a norm for most of the pilgrimage but ultimately degenerates in a way that calls into question its adequacy as a means of communication. What he creates is an image not just of how fictions function within society but how social discourse operates within and moves between the secular and the sacred. There is no simple formula to explain how the *Canterbury Tales* enacts that movement, particularly at the end. The game as initially established provides a set of respectable social norms, though easily subject to abuse or disruption. Occasionally a passage reminds us of what lies beyond the game. In Fragment IX the behavior of the company turns cynical and offensive, and in Fragment X the Parson speaks with hostility toward the telling of fables. He seems to reject the game, to point to another kind of discourse. But his speaking too is a *tale,* and for all his self-separation from what has preceded, the pilgrims agree that he should end the storytelling; they see his particular kind of wisdom as appropriate, not discontinuous. The Parson's Tale is both somehow within and beyond the game, and in spite of what happens in Fragment IX the structure implies that there is at least some common ground between the earlier fictions and his own. . . . The final complexity of Chaucer's Canterbury game is the difficulty of knowing when it's over, of knowing, even in the face of his Retraction, how sharply to distinguish the worldly vanity from the devotion.

The Use of the Narrator in *The Canterbury Tales*

Dieter Mehl

Many scholars have commented on Chaucer's frequent use of the narrator as a literary device in his
works. In this essay, Chaucer expert Dieter Mehl, a
professor at Germany's University of Bonn, makes
the point that in *The Canterbury Tales* Chaucer uses
various narrators, along with the act of storytelling
those narrators engage in, as a unifying concept, a
way of pulling together the work's many and diverse
characters and tales. In the Prologue to the *Tales*, according to Mehl, the narrator's chief concern is simply to identify the pilgrims who will be making the
journey to Canterbury. This initial narrator is a self-
assured, educated man much like Chaucer himself.
Later in the work, many other narrators appear, several of them a good deal less like Chaucer, and each
with his or her own storytelling style. Indeed, says
Mehl, Chaucer seems to have deliberately constructed a complex network of diverse storytellers,
his purpose being not only to entertain his readers,
but also to make them think.

Chaucer's narrator is the discovery of a fairly recent generation of critics. Earlier readers had, of course, noticed the very
personal tone of most of Chaucer's poems, but it had not really occurred to them to make a consistent distinction between Geoffrey Chaucer the poet and the 'I' speaking in his
works. Modern theories of narrative, however, most influen-
tial among them Wayne Booth's *The Rhetoric of Fiction*, have
pointed out that there is such a thing as an 'unreliable narrator' and that it is very unsophisticated if not misleading to
identify the narrator with the author. This approach was first
of all applied to the modern novel, where it certainly led to a

Dieter Mehl, "Chaucer's Narrator," in *The Cambridge Chaucer Companion*, edited by
Piero Boitani and Jill Mann (New York: Cambridge University Press, 1986). Copyright
©1986 by Cambridge University Press. Reprinted by permission of Cambridge University Press.

much better understanding of many texts, but it also seemed helpful in reading earlier authors, and for a time the analysis of narrators became a fashionable critical occupation, which yielded many valuable insights, but was (as often happens with critical fashions) sometimes overdone. . . .

The most interesting aspect of Chaucer's narrator is not what he reveals about the author's personal life and opinions, but the way he directs our responses and controls the narrative situation. This is observable as early as the *Book of the Duchess* whose 'obtuse' narrator has been subjected to subtle analysis more than once. He tells us one or two intriguing things about himself, such as the fact of his eight years' sickness. It seems an obvious reference to unsuccessful love, but whether it is a conventional pose, or a personal confession his first audience would know how to interpret, will, I suppose, always remain a mystery.

More important is the function of this narrator for the effect of the whole poem; he is a sympathetic listener, and his brief expression of condolence after the Black Knight's elaborate account of his suffering strikes the reader as a genuine and spontaneous attempt to share the bereaved lover's despair. The narrator is a far more individualized figure than many of the conventional dreamers, and the same applies to Chaucer's other dream-allegories, such as the *House of Fame*, the *Parliament of Fowls*, and the *Legend of Good Women*. In all these poems, the poet presents himself as a rather bookish, impractical person whose knowledge of love and of poetry comes from reading rather than from experience and who is granted a sight of the 'real thing' without getting actively involved in the service of love. . . .

COMPETING NARRATORS

When we turn to the *Canterbury Tales*, the problem of the narrator is quite different because there is such a variety of narrators, none of them quite like the other, yet all of them obviously concerned with the art of telling a story. From the start, when the Host promises a dinner to the most successful narrator, there is an element of competition, and indeed, every narrator gives the impression of trying to do his best. Critics will go on disagreeing about the extent to which each tale has to be read as the performance of a particular narrator; but there cannot be any doubt about the prominence of the narrative situation throughout the whole collection.

Story-telling is the subject of this unfinished compilation as much as any of the themes that are taken up by pilgrims in their tales or any of the general 'ideas' that have been suggested as unifying concepts.

THE NARRATOR APOLOGIZES FOR HIS SHORTCOMINGS

In this excerpt from Vincent F. Hopper's modernized translation of the Prologue to the Tales, *the author-narrator begs the reader to bear with him and to forgive the plainness and crudeness of the descriptions that will follow.*

Now have I told you briefly, in a sentence,
The status, the clothes, the number, and also the cause
Of the gathering of this company
In Southwark, at this fine hotel,
Named the Tabard, close to the Bell Inn.
But now it is time to tell you
What we did that same night,
On which we arrived at that hotel.
And afterwards I will tell of our journey,
And everything else about our pilgrimage.
But first I beg you, out of your courtesy,
That you ascribe it not to my crudeness,
Even though I speak plainly in this narration,
To tell you their words and their behavior;
Even if I repeat their exact words.
For this you know as well as I,
Whoever tells another man's story,
Must reproduce, as exactly as he can,
Every word, if his memory serves,
However vulgar and broad his language;
Or else he must falsify his tale,
Or invent things, or find new words.

. . . .

Also I beg you to forgive me
If I have not placed people in their rank,
Here in this tale, in the order that they should be;
My brains are weak, you can well understand.

Apart from the pilgrim-narrators, briefly characterized in the *General Prologue* and the links between tales, but above all by their contributions to the story-telling contest, there is, of course, Chaucer himself as the narrator of the whole collection, and he appears in various guises: he is, first of all, one of the pilgrims who introduces us to the company, describes his fellow travellers, and proceeds to give an account of the story-telling. This aspect of the narrator has had more than its fair share of attention: the narrator of the *General Prologue* has been called a satirist and a naive innocent, but I do not think he is really meant to be a very distinct personality who might distract the reader from the real subject of this introduction. The narrator is not the recipient of important revelations, as is the 'I' in the dream visions, and his chief concern is to describe the pilgrims to us. There is, of course, a fair amount of subversive irony in these portraits of cheats, rogues, and hypocrites, but the remarkable thing is that the satire is so gentle and indirect and that the narrator most of the time lets the characters speak for themselves rather than unmasking them with the satirist's proper anger or scorn.

The narrator presents himself as a sociable person who is able to find out the relevant facts about more than twenty fellow pilgrims in the course of an evening, but also as an author who promises to give us all the details in their appropriate order. . . .

A THIN LINE BETWEEN POET AND NARRATOR

Once the story-telling contest has begun in earnest, there are only two other places where the narrator becomes a more prominent part of the fiction. He is addressed by the Host in a way that suggests again the bookish and unsociable 'Geffrey' of the *House of Fame*, and, unlike any of the other pilgrims, he is given the chance to tell two stories, one after the other—stories that represent the two extremes of oral and literary narrative, of popular entertainment and bookish instruction. Modest and shy as the author appears to the Host, his two contributions give an impression of complete self-assurance and of wide literary interests. The *Tale of Sir Thopas* can be appreciated only by a reader who is thoroughly familiar with the clichés of popular romance, and it is obvious that the Host fails to see the point of this brilliant parody. The text does not make quite clear how seriously the pilgrim-narrator himself takes this ridiculous story; but there is certainly no deliberate impression of an unreliable narrator nor any reason to doubt that this narrator, like Chaucer himself, knows what he is doing. . . . Whatever else the author's own two contributions to the story-telling contest achieve, they draw attention to the literary aspects of this mixed collection and to his stylistic versatility. Again, the narrator is not presented as an individualized character in his own right, but primarily as a writer and story-teller.

This also applies to his most personal and appealing appearance in the whole work, that is, the *Retractions* at the very end. Here the concept of the 'unreliable narrator' breaks down completely. No sensitive reader would seriously suggest that Chaucer is here talking tongue in cheek, and yet it would be much too simple to take the *Retractions* as a straightforward confession or even a sign of Chaucer's final conversion. It is, after all, not a public circular, sent round to all the owners and readers of Chaucer's Collected Works, but an integral part of the work, copied along with all the other stories in most of the important manuscripts. It is, therefore, part of the fiction, an utterance by the narrator, not by the man Geoffrey Chaucer. Within the fictional world of the *Canterbury Tales*, it is one and the same author-narrator who in the *General Prologue* addresses us. . . .

The *Retractions* is not, then, a wholesale repudiation of his poetry or an attempt to cancel what he had written, but a final appeal to the reader to make the proper use of the author's labours and to reflect on the powerful vitality of literature for good or evil. The narrator is, until the last, deeply concerned about the effect of his book on the reader. Indeed, the moral responsibility of authors and the close interrelationship between teller, tale, and audience are among the most prominent themes of the *Canterbury Tales* and Chaucer's brilliant use of narrators is a significant contribution to the debate on these themes implied in the story-telling contest.

A DIVERSITY OF STYLES

The poet as narrator is but one aspect of it; another is the provocative diversity of story-tellers and of narrative styles. This is a large and complex subject because the interpretation of each tale depends, of course, on the importance we attach to the narrative situation and the narrator's reliability, but I think very few of the *Canterbury Tales* can be read without some awareness of their narrators, if we are not to ignore an important part of their full meaning. It is evident that Chaucer was particularly interested in the problem of 'unreliable' narrators and that he experimented ingeniously with various possibilities and with degrees of subjectivity.

The most obvious instances are the unguarded confessions of villains, like the Pardoner, or figures of fun, like the Wife of Bath, where it is impossible to miss the satiric effect produced by this form of first-person narrative. The reader knows all the time that the 'I' of these confessions is not the author and that he or she is not to be trusted or at least not to be taken seriously. We never forget the speakers, as we read these remarkable revelations, and though we may disagree about the violence or the consistency of the satire, we never fall into the error of taking these narrators at their word without keeping our critical distance.

This also applies, though perhaps not to the same extent, to their actual tales. It is an important function of these unashamed confessions to alert the reader to the highly subjective character of most individual utterances and to sharpen our ears for misplaced emphasis, exaggerated pathos, empty rhetoric, or faulty reasoning. Thus, many stylistic devices that would be perfectly normal and innocent in a different context, suddenly take on a more complex meaning because we see them in relation to other modes of expression and begin to question their sincerity and their innocence. It is, of course, very easy for the modern reader to be too sophisticated in this respect, and Saul Bellow's warning, 'Deep Readers of the World, Beware!' is as relevant for Chaucer-critics as it is for obsessive irony-hunters in other fields of literature. Yet the stylistic contrasts and the degrees of refinement, intelligence, and tolerance within the *Canterbury Tales* are so obvious that it is hard to believe they were not meant to reflect degrees of insight and credibility and to keep us constantly aware of the fact that all the narrators, like the author, represent but single and necessarily limited points of view. . . .

TEASING THE READER'S IMAGINATION

Many of the links between the tales are tantalizingly brief, and the textual situation often does not even allow us to say confidently which tales are meant to be linked or who the speakers are; but by and large, all the surviving fragments of the frame [the overall work] add further substance to the fiction of a succession of narrative situations and a provocative diversity of stylistic attitudes. It is in this sense that the question of the fictitious narrator is so important for our appreciation of Chaucer's narrative art. This does not mean that the poet himself is only a completely detached observer without any convictions of his own. . . . What it does mean is that Chaucer is far more interested in the complex relationships between story-material, author, reader, and personal style than he is in straightforward instruction and unambiguous authorial statement. Whether there are any of the *Canterbury Tales* he would have 'released' separately, in his own name as it were, is a rather hypothetical but not quite irrelevant question. None of the over twenty narrators is to be identified with Chaucer himself as we believe we know him, though some are more like him than others, such as the Clerk, the Knight, the Man of Law, and, perhaps, the Franklin, and nearly all of them share characteristic elements of style, hard to define but unmistakably present. This makes it very difficult to decide on the precise degree of subjectivity in any particular case and is one of the chief reasons for such contradictory interpretations of many tales. If we think of the Prioress as an exemplary representative of her estate and a thoroughly reliable narrator, we shall probably read the *Prioress's Tale* as an unexceptional miracle, but if we consider her portrait to be a satirical attack on a rather too worldly and hypocritical woman we are likely to mistrust her narrative too and begin to wonder whether it is meant as a parody of childish legends or something even more sinister. The alternatives are usually much more subtle than this, and Chaucer's narrative technique is playfully experimental rather than neatly consistent, alerting the reader to the possibility of subversive irony and teasing him into imaginative mental cooperation. It is not surprising that our reaction to many of the tales is no more unanimous than that of the Canterbury pilgrims themselves, nor is complete critical agreement desirable in reading texts that so clearly encourage discussion and reflection rather than certainty and mere receptiveness.

ASSUMING A VARIETY OF ROLES

Perhaps the problem is most acute in the case of the Parson and his tale, though most critics and readers are not particularly interested in this last item of the collection. Since the *Parson's Tale* is not really a tale at all, but rather a prose tract, it hardly seems to make sense to speak of a narrator. From what we are told about the Parson, he is an 'estate ideal' and we expect a truly edifying tale from him. In a way, his sermon on penitence is a most fitting summary and conclusion to all that has gone before, but it does not devalue it, just as the Parson's portrait in the *General Prologue* fails to upset the confident tone in which the skills of the *Prologue*'s rogues are presented. The unsophisticated moral seriousness of the speaker and his undiluted homily are only another possibility of story-telling, no less subjective and relative than the rest, though obviously more worthy of imitation. Like the *Retractions*, the *Parson's Tale* is not the definite and authoritative answer to everything else in the book, but an offer we may accept or reject. . . . In this sense, the Parson is a narrator like the rest of his fellow pilgrims. . . .

Even to the last, Chaucer does not turn his back on this literary principle of individual viewpoints and personal responsibility. It is the final demonstration of the poet-narrator assuming a variety of roles in his constant search for the most effective way of appealing to his audience.

The Symbolic Time Frame of the Canterbury Journey

Sigmund Eisner

One structural concept Chaucer had to keep in mind throughout his writing of the Canterbury collection is the passage of time the pilgrims experience on their journey. His expression of time passing and of the duration of the trek could have been meant to be taken either literally or symbolically. In this essay, University of Arizona scholar Sigmund Eisner advocates the symbolic option, arguing that a real journey from Southwark to Canterbury in Chaucer's time took about four days, while in the text of the *Tales* the pilgrimage is completed in a single day. Therefore, says Eisner, Chaucer was describing a metaphysical, spiritual journey more than a real one. The essay also graphically illustrates the fact that dozens of noted scholars over hundreds of years will minutely examine and vigorously debate a single literary point out of the many thousands that make up the work's framework and text.

Has no one remarked that once they leave Southwark, Chaucer's Canterbury Pilgrims never sleep? They eat, they drink, they quarrel, and they tell stories. But not once is it said that they go to bed and sleep although just before the Manciple tells his tale the Cook is caught napping on his horse by the ever-vigilant Host. Most scholars, however, assume that the Pilgrims spend their nights at Dartford, Rochester, and Ospringe, thus occupying four days on the journey. The purpose of this paper is to challenge the view that the Pilgrims travel more than a single day and to propose a given anagogical [mystical or symbolic] day for the journey.

The four-day journey is relatively new in Chaucer schol-

From Sigmund Eisner, "Canterbury Day: A Fresh Aspect," *Chaucer Review*, vol. 27, no. 1, 1992, pp. 31-44. Copyright 1992 by The Pennsylvania State University. Reproduced by permission of the Pennsylvania State University Press.

arship. Thomas Tyrwhitt [an English classical scholar] in 1775 spoke of "the day of the journey to Canterbury." It did not occur to him that the Pilgrims travel for more than a single day. Arthur Penrhyr Stanley in 1854, then a canon of the Canterbury Cathedral and later Dean of Westminster, admitted to the one-day journey but appeared to be uneasy about it: "The journey, although at that time usually occupying three or four days, is compressed into the hours between sunrise and sunset on an April day." In 1868 Frederick J. Furnivall, the intrepid founder of the Chaucer Society as well as several other literary societies, divided the fifty-four-mile trip as follows: Day 1, leave Southwark in morning, travel for fifteen miles, and spend the night at Dartford. Day 2, travel another fifteen miles to Rochester. Day 3, travel ten miles to Sittingbourne for a meal and continue six more miles to Ospringe for a night's sleep. Day 4, complete the eight miles to Canterbury. Furnivall based the Pilgrims' itinerary on two [documented journeys]: the first by the dowager Queen Isabella of England in 1358 and the second by King John II of France in 1360. On both of these journeys sleeping arrangements were made at Dartford, Rochester, and Ospringe, and King John is recorded as having enjoyed a meal at Sittingbourne. On reading these itineraries Furnivall declared: "After this we may fairly assume that the regular sleeping-places on the road were *Dartford, Rochester, Ospringe*, and that Chaucer and his fellow Pilgrims were three or four days on their journey."

In a persuasive 1894 argument W.W. Skeat [an English literary scholar] endorsed Furnivall's scheme of a four-day journey: "Any one who knows what travelling was in the olden time must be well aware that the notion of performing the whole distance in one day is out of the question, especially as the pilgrims were out more for a holiday than for business, that some of them were but poorly mounted, and some of them but poor riders. In fact, such an idea is purely modern, adopted from thoughtlessness almost as a matter of course by many modern readers, but certainly not founded upon truth." So overwhelming are the reputations of both Furnivall and Skeat that hardly anyone has resurrected the one-day journey. These nineteenth-century scholars were right, I am sure, when they asserted that historical travelers in the fourteenth century did not attempt the London or Southwark journey to Canterbury in a single day. But the *Canterbury Tales* is not an historical document. It is a work of art, and that, indeed, is strikingly different from factual history.

Furnivall, Skeat, and others, schooled in the fiction of their times, required realistic probability in all literature and so sought rationally historical verisimilitude [reality] in the Canterbury Pilgrimage. For it is certainly reasonable to assume that devout fourteenth-century pilgrims on their way to a noted shrine would not race to their goal but would in a leisurely manner entertain each other with tales which perhaps they had heard on other pilgrimages or in other social situations. The realism is increased by Chaucer's detailed portraits of the Pilgrims and their very human reactions to each other. But . . . the verisimilitude which comforted Furnivall and Skeat is only frosting on a very rich cake. Furthermore, it does not always hold up. On the night before the Pilgrimage Chaucer describes the Pilgrims with intimate details impossible to know on such short acquaintanceship: the Friar's financial manipulations, the Merchant's secret indebtedness, the Clerk's bedside reading, and the Reeve's livestock. In addition, he describes how most of them are mounted, even though their horses are secure in the stable of the Tabard Inn and out of Chaucer's line of vision. [Scholar] W.W. Lawrence wisely stated in 1950 that it would be impossible for thirty-odd Pilgrims, each mounted and traveling, to attend and comprehend a story told by one of themselves. Even if they are riding in double file, the Pilgrimage might stretch at least one hundred yards along the road. A reader of the *Canterbury Tales*, like the readers of most great poetry, must suspend disbelief and disabuse himself or herself of the assumption that Chaucer's creation is factual history. There is, as scholars for the past forty years have pointed out, something far more significant here. . . .

DETERMINING THE TIME OF DAY

At the start of the journey Chaucer says that the Host of the Tabard Inn rises at the very beginning of morning twilight in order to call the other Pilgrims. . . .

At the end of the journey we are told that the day is drawing to a close and that the sun is sinking. . . . It does not matter here that the Dowager Queen Isabella of England and King John II of France spent four days on road from London to Canterbury. Chaucer's Canterbury Pilgrims are not ordinary travelers. They represent devout Christians on the *via bona* [the good way, or heavenly road] to the New Jerusalem [heaven, or salvation], and their anagogical journey is framed by eternity, by their own lives, and by the solar passage from sunrise to sunset. Thus the extent of the Canterbury journey may be studied simultaneously as the time from Creation to Doomsday, as a lifetime, and as a single day.

Specific references within the text of the *Canterbury Tales* endorse the single day's journey. One must first assume that between Southwark and Canterbury geographical sites are named in the order in which one would come to them, for the spiritual pilgrimage may be set along a familiar road. The actual places named are the Watering of Saint Thomas, about two miles out; Deptford, five miles out; Greenwich, a half mile from Deptford; Rochester, about thirty miles from Southwark; Sittingbourne, about forty miles along the way; Boughton, about forty-nine miles out; and Harbledown, about fifty-two miles from Southwark and two miles from Canterbury. The most frequently used manuscript of the *Canterbury Tales*, the Ellesmere, offers an order of the tales which violates the geographical sequence of the mentioned sites, for in this manuscript the positions of Rochester and Sittingbourne are reversed. The fact is that at his death Chaucer left his tales in individual gatherings which were eventually placed together in whatever order pleased the compiler. Many editors in the past two centuries, however, have been so pleased with the excellence of the Ellesmere manuscript that, although they acknowledge that its order of the places visited is nonsequential, they have nevertheless retained it. Other editors, however, have attempted to correct the order of tales to insure geographic verisimilitude. In 1868 Furnivall said that Henry Bradshaw, the Librarian of Cambridge University Library, had suggested that the gathering containing the reference to Rochester be moved to a place prior to the gathering containing the reference to Sittingbourne. Furnivall's delighted reaction to this proposal has been quoted often, but one more time will do no harm to the thesis of this essay: "A happy hit! And it sets us free to alter the arrangement of any or all of the MSS [manuscript] to move up or down any *Groups* of Tales, whenever internal evidence, probability, or presumption, requires it." Furnivall, who generously gave Bradshaw full credit for the innovation, not only followed Bradshaw's suggestion but unilaterally [on his own] altered the position of another fragment to help prove that the journey takes four days, thus following his own intuition, in which he had far more confidence than have present scholars. Furnivall's order of tales appeared in the Chaucer Society edition, and Skeat carried it forward into his own six-volume edition of 1894, which later became the source of the Oxford *Chaucer's Works.* In a thoughtful 1951 essay, [Chaucerian scholar] Robert A. Pratt analyzed all possible orders of the *Canterbury Tales,* agreed with Bradshaw's suggestion, but rejected Furnivall's unilateral alteration. The Pratt order seems to me to be the most logical and also the most workable. . . .

Using the Pratt order, we can, I think, trace the Canterbury Day from early morning, when the Pilgrims leave Southwark, to early evening, when the Parson begins his tale. For reasons that I hope to establish below, I am assuming that the date is the same date mentioned in the Headlink to the *Man of Law's Tale:* 18 April. The Pilgrims had retired the previous night at the Tabard Inn in Southwark. On the morning of the journey the Host, in order to wake the others, rises at the beginning of the morning twilight . . . 2:17 A.M. The Pilgrims are on their way by sunrise, which is 4:47 A.M. It is still early morning when the Host indicates that they are at Deptford and that the time is "half-wey pryme." Prime normally means the end of the third hour of the day. . . .

Since sunrise on 18 April . . . is 4:47 A.M., and noon is always the midpoint of the day, sunset has to be 7:13 P.M. The time from sunrise to sunset or the artificial day is 14 hours, 26 minutes. One canonical hour would be on that day about 1 hour and 12 minutes. That amount multiplied by three and added to the time of sunrise would yield prime at about 8:23 "of the clokke." Half prime by the same calculations would be 6:35 A.M. Later in the Pilgrimage in the Headlink to the *Man of Law's Tale* the time is noted as "ten of the clokke," and by the time we reach the *Prologue* to the *Parson's Tale,* the time is "Foure of the clokke." The implication, although there is not as yet ironclad proof, is that the Pilgrimage takes place on a given day. . . .

THE YEAR OF THE PILGRIMAGE

The year of the Canterbury Pilgrimage is another matter entirely. It must not be confused with the year of Chaucer's composition, for it is generally agreed that Chaucer wrote parts of the *Canterbury Tales* at different times during his ca-

reer. Nor must it be confused with any actual Canterbury
pilgrimage which may be uncovered by astute historians
who discover that living personages such as Geoffrey
Chaucer or Harry Bailly did indeed go to Canterbury. I am
interested, however, in the symbolic year in which the proposed one-day journey occurs. The year may be limited by
historical references; Chaucer could not have discussed a
known event before its occurrence or after his own death.
But it must be remembered that the mention of an historical
event offers neither a date of composition nor a proposed
date for the Pilgrimage. The best that it offers us is historical
boundaries for the time of composition. [Scholar] J.W. Hales
in 1893 argued that because the Merchant wishes the sea to
be kept clear between Orwell in England and Middelburg in
Holland, ports licensed to ship and receive wool only during
the years 1384–1388, Chaucer must have composed the portrait of the Merchant, and presumably the entire *General
Prologue*, during those years. At best this . . . tells us very little about the date of composition, about any historical pilgrimage, or about one particular symbolic pilgrimage. Skeat
in 1894, assuming that during Easter week the Parson's duties would keep him at home, proposed the year 1387. . . .

In 1916 Albert S. Cook [an American expert on early English literature] in a challenge to the 1387 date of Pilgrimage,
observed that some of the travels of Chaucer's Knight, as out-
lined in the *General Prologue*, are similar to several Baltic
expeditions made between 1390 and 1393 by Henry, Earl of
Derby, the future King Henry IV of England. Cook concluded
that since Henry did not return from his last trip to the Baltic
until 1393, the *General Prologue* was written after that
time. . . . I agree with Cook that a post-1390 date must be a
terminus a quo [starting point] for the Canterbury Pilgrimage and also for the composition of the part of the *General
Prologue* which includes the Knight's northern adventures.
From 1385 until 1388, because of deteriorated relations between England and the Hanseatic League of Prussia, the
English were forbidden by their own government to travel to
the Baltic. In August 1390, two years after a treaty between
England and the Teutonic Order, which represented the
Hanseatic League, Henry first journeyed to Prussia and
Lithuania, where he landed near Danzig and marched to
one successful battle and then to the unsuccessful siege of
Vilna or modern Vilnius. . . . All authorities agree that

"Pruce" [mentioned in the *Knight's Tale*] is Prussia and "Lettow" is Lithuania. . . . Because this expedition occurred in August 1390, 1391 must stand as a *terminus a quo* for the Canterbury Year.

FORTUNATE PLANETARY POSITIONS

Hales, Cook, and their followers give us historical boundaries for the Canterbury Pilgrimage, and in our search for a Canterbury Day, we would be wise to stay within them. The only actual date mentioned within the framework to the *Canterbury Tales* is 18 April. In 1976 and again in 1980 I hesitatingly suggested, without any real corroborative evidence, that the symbolic year of the Canterbury Pilgrimage (not the year of composition) is 1394 because 19 April is Easter Sunday in that year. I think now that the climactic celebration of the salvation of the Pilgrims should rightfully occur on such a date. Easter Sunday must be the beginning of Purgatory for the Pilgrims just as it is for Dante [the medieval Italian author of the *Divine Comedy*], who enters Purgatory at dawn on Easter Sunday, 10 April 1300, the very moment commemorating Christ's resurrection. Chaucer, familiar with both the *Divine Comedy* and the Gospels, could not be unaware of such a chronological metaphor and is quite capable of incorporating it into the *Canterbury Tales.*

The suggested parallel to Dante, however, is still not iron-clad evidence for the date of 18 April 1394. Nor is a symbolic 1394 date for the Canterbury Pilgrimage commonly accepted or even considered by most Chaucer scholars.

It occurred to me that it might be a reasonable exercise to see if 18 April 1394 is a more astrologically propitious day for travel than any other 17 or 18 April from 1391 through 1400. . . .

Although there is no evidence that Chaucer himself subscribes to astrology any more than he does to pagan beliefs and much evidence that he does not, he is capable of using astrology for artistic purposes. His Man of Law complains that no astrologer at the court of the Roman Emperor foresaw the difficulties faced by Custance, his daughter, when she embarked on her journey to the land of the pagans. One must conclude that it was the Man of Law and not his creator who believes in astrology. The Wife of Bath confesses that Mars and Venus inclined her at birth toward her aggressive lechery, that she always follows her inclination, and that it coincides with her appetite. Although the Franklin condemns astrology as folly contrary to the teachings of the Church, he does introduce us to a character who has a knowledgeable acquaintance with astrology. . . . The conclusion is inescapable that Chaucer, and his audience also, were familiar enough with the tenets of astrology so that if Chaucer chooses an astrologically propitious day for the Canterbury Pilgrimage, the choice is deliberate and should not go unnoticed.

In astrology a day is propitious for a journey if the Moon is applying (that is, approaching) a favorable aspect (which is an angle of sextile, that is 60°, or trine, that is 120°, on the zodiac) with Jupiter and then with any other planet. Furthermore the favor is increased if the Moon is in Sagittarius, which is a sign associated with travel. These points have been known to astrologers since they were set down by [the Alexandrian scholar] Claudius Ptolemy in the second century, A.D. . . . On 18 April 1394 the Moon at sunrise was at 28° 57' of Scorpio. Before 10:00 A.M. it had entered Sagittarius. At 4:00 P.M. it was about at 5° of Sagittarius, and by sunset it was near 6° of Sagittarius. Also at sunrise Mercury was at 9° 53' of Aries, Venus at 16° 44' of Aries, Mars 10° 14' of Aries, Jupiter 11° 15' of Aries, and Saturn at 24° 27' of Libra. Three planets, Mars, Jupiter, and Mercury, were clustered within a degree of each other; that is, they were in a triple and most unusual conjunction. Venus was close enough to the other three to be considered in platic conjunction. It becomes evident that at one given time of one given historical day the Moon was applying an aspect of 120° with not only Jupiter but also Mercury, Venus, and Mars. Also, the Moon entered Sagittarius on that date, and the Moon in Sagittarius, as I said above, brings fortune to travelers. . . . In summary, the Moon was, according to fourteenth-century astrology, in favorable aspect with Mercury, Venus, Mars, Jupiter, and Saturn. A more favorable moment for a journey did not exist in any other day appropriate for the Pilgrimage. In fact, I am willing to venture that such a fortunate time for a journey did not exist in any other day of the fourteenth century.

Sunrise on 18 April 1394 was just about as propitious for a journey as any moment of any day could be. On no other appropriate day between 1391 and 1400 were the positions of the planets so favorable for travel. Joyce L. Taylor, a Professional Member of the American Federation of Astrologers, a professional astrologer who explained to me the astrological information presented here, said, "This is the most fortunate time for a journey that I have ever noted in my fifteen years as an astrologer." Her statement was confirmed by another astrologer. The way to Canterbury on that date was indeed a *via bona.* In fact, I would not hesitate to call it a *via bonissima* [best way]. . . .

ON THE PATH TO PARADISE

Neither Chaucer nor his audience would have been unaware that the day before Easter in 1394 was, according to all astrological indicators, an extraordinarily propitious day for traveling. Nor would Chaucer have been unaware that Dante took his own anagogical journey during Holy Week, achieving the beginning of Purgatory at dawn on Easter Sunday. Although Chaucer does not bring his Pilgrims into the city limits of Canterbury, they are so close at dusk on 18 April that one must assume that at sunrise on Easter Sunday, 19 April 1394, the traditional moment of the Resurrection, the Canterbury Pilgrims, sinners all, are in Canterbury and ready, like Dante, for their own resurrections to begin with their journey through Purgatory on the tortuous paths to their assigned places in Paradise.

So we see why the Canterbury Pilgrims do not sleep after that early morning in Southwark. . . . The Pilgrims are traveling on the most significant journey of their lives, on their way to the New Jerusalem, along the road to Canterbury, where they are scheduled to begin the purgation of their sins at dawn on Easter morning, 19 April 1394.

Chaucer's Language and Verse

M.W. Grose

In this excerpt from his book *Chaucer*, M.W. Grose, a noted expert on Old and Middle English language and literature, explains how English words and grammar have steadily changed over the course of decades and centuries. In particular, he shows how many of the words Chaucer used now have different spellings and pronunciations, and even different meanings. Grose also discusses the rhythm of Chaucer's verse, using a section of the General Prologue to *The Canterbury Tales* as an example. There are two competing theories, he points out, about where the stresses on these lines should fall and, therefore, how someone should read the lines aloud; yet no matter which version a reader chooses, he or she can still understand and enjoy Chaucer's sharp and witty observations of people and everyday life.

The difficulty to a modern reader of Chaucer's English arises from the way in which all languages are constantly changing. When we consider how little of a modern conversation would have been fully understood by, say, [the English poet, Alfred Lord] Tennyson, only a hundred years ago, and when we consider that Tennyson is now being extensively annotated by scholars (though it is easier for us to understand him than he us) we can appreciate Chaucer's remarks on this very problem [in *Troilus and Criseyde*]:

> Ye knowe ek that in forme of speche is chaunge
> Withinne a thousand yeer, and wordes tho
> That hadden pris, now wonder nyce and straunge
> Us thinketh hem, and yet thei spake hem so
> And spedde as wel in love as men now do. . . .

Observe also that this passage illustrates some of the difficulties produced by changes in the language. There are ob-

From M.W. Grose, *Chaucer* (New York: Arco, 1969), pp. 84-96.

solete words (*ek*, also, and *tho*, then); obsolete syntax—*us thinketh* is not just bad grammar for 'we think'; it is an impersonal construction—'it seems to us'—which is a survival from an earlier period of the language; and, most important and most difficult of all, there are words which are still recognizable, but whose meanings have changed completely in the past six centuries: *nice* is one of the most notorious examples of this in English. Ultimately it derives from the Latin *nescio* ('I am ignorant of') by way of French, but down through the centuries its meaning has gradually changed through 'unknown', 'strange' (its meaning in this passage), 'rare', 'tender', 'delicate', 'fastidious', 'precise', 'refined', 'cultured', 'agreeable', and finally to its indefinable modern usage in which we apply it to anything we vaguely approve of, from a nice girl to a nice dinner.

These changes since Chaucer's time have occurred in the first two-thirds of his 'thousand yeer', but the history of English stretches back as far beyond Chaucer as he is distant from us. His language is only one stage of continuous development, and because he happened to live at one of the more important periods of this development, it will probably help if I briefly sketch in the history of our language from Old English, through Middle English to the beginnings of the language we speak today.

OLD ENGLISH

Old English, as the term implies, is the oldest period in the history of the language; it extended until about a century after the Norman Conquest [or to the mid–twelfth century]. Middle English continued until the end of the 15th century; from then on is what we call Modern English. (The reader will realize, of course, that these three terms are created by scholars for the purposes of analysis and discussion, and will not think that they imply that sudden changes took place in 1166 or 1499, but merely that it is convenient to talk of the English of King Alfred's time as Old English, and that this is manifestly different in certain definable and obvious ways from the Middle English of Chaucer and his contemporaries.)

The beginnings lie back in the 5th and 6th centuries A.D. when Britain was invaded by a group of related Germanic tribes. Bede, the first English historian, writing of course in Latin, at the beginning of the 8th century, says that the invaders were three of the most formidable tribes of Germans: the Angles, the Saxons and the Jutes. The Jutes settled in Kent and the Isle of Wight, the Saxons in the rest of the south and south-west, and the Angles in the Midlands and the north of England. The Jutes have gone unremembered; but the Angles and the Saxons gave their name to Anglo-Saxon, the now old-fashioned name for Old English. . . . These groups naturally differed somewhat in their speech, and from these differences spring the various dialects of today; but they had enough in common to form a new branch, English (Anglish), of the Germanic family of languages, as they developed in isolation from their cousins on the Continent.

The next invaders also spoke a related Germanic language; starting in the closing years of the 8th century and continuing in the 9th century, there were several waves of Scandinavian adventurers who came first merely to plunder, but later stayed to settle. . . . Their effect on the English language does not show itself till after the Norman Conquest, when the way in which Scandinavian words were adopted argues for a mingling of the two peoples. . . . This is a rather more detached view of the Norman Conquest than our own, which is coloured by our descent also from the invaders, so that we tend to forget that in 1066 an alien way of life was imposed from above by foreigners speaking an entirely different language—for French is one of the group of languages directly descended from Latin, while the Germanic family of languages certainly is not.

Because, unlike the Danes and Norsemen, the Normans had control of the central government, introduced their own aristocracy, and occupied all the positions of high office, French displaced English as the language of government, just as English was to be used throughout the British Empire and is still used even when British rule has ceased and in cases where all other connection with Britain is severed.

English was of course still spoken by the bulk of the population; the racial distinction between the use of English and French must soon have turned into a social one, for the upper classes governed in French while everybody else went about their business in English. There is evidence, too, that French was used officially for long after it had ceased to be the native tongue of the nobility, and that by the 14th century those who could speak French were certainly bilingual. . . .

MIDDLE ENGLISH

The English that [eventually] came into official use was by now quite different from that which was spoken before the Norman Conquest. Old English is an inflected language, like Latin, in which the relationship between the words in a sentence is shown by their form. Middle English, the new official language, is more like modern German; it has lost most of the inflections and in consequence is much more dependent upon prepositions and word order to show the construction of the sentence. In one way this makes it easier for us to read a Middle English author like Chaucer, because the general pattern of his sentences is like our own; but in another way we can be caught out by survivals of older forms which we may not expect because externally they look just like our own modern ones. Take, for example, 'his hors were goode', in the description of the Knight from the *General Prologue*. *Hors* appears to us to be singular—it is not until we reach *were* that we realize it must be plural; and in less obvious examples we can be badly led astray. Another case of a noun, which, for historical linguistic reasons, is uninflected where we would expect an inflection in Modern English, is *lady* in the phrase from the description of the Squire: 'to stonden in his lady grace'. This uninflected genitive, common to feminine nouns in Old English, survives today only in set phrases like *Lady Day*; elsewhere the feminine nouns of Modern English have adopted the *'s* for the genitive by analogy with the masculine nouns.

Secondly, Middle English acquired a vast number of foreign words, particularly from the French- and Scandinavian-speaking invaders. The borrowings from the French reflect, to a considerable degree, the social position of the French. The language of government, law, military affairs and the Church depends heavily on French words. A short list may show this: *Parliament, government, crown, empire, sovereign, statute, tax, exchequer, chancellor, treasurer*, are all French in origin, and so too are all titles of rank apart from the native *king, queen, lord, lady* and *earl*; this reflects, no doubt, the decimation of the English nobility at the time of the Conquest. In law, *justice, crime, judgement, plaintiff, defendant, bail, bar, assize, verdict*, are all French. And, turning to more domestic matters, it is pleasant to speculate, as did Sir Walter Scott in *Ivanhoe*, that the modern words for dead meat, ready for consumption, come from the French, while the words for the live animals are all English, because it was the French-speakers who would be able to eat meat more often and who saw it on the table instead of on the hoof. At any rate, we still have the pairs *cow/beef; sheep/mutton; pig/pork; calf/veal; deer/venison.* . . .

Thirdly, the relative importance of the dialects had changed. By the end of the Old English period, West Saxon, the dialect of King Alfred's capital, Winchester, had become the standard literary language. After the Conquest, when for a time English was restricted to the uneducated, there was no longer such a thing as Standard English. Gradually, however, from the 14th century onwards the East Midlands dialect of London asserted itself, and became the ancestor of the Standard English of today. It had the great advantage of being the dialect of the seat of government, of the most populous area of the county, and of the two universities, Oxford and Cambridge; and finally, it had the prestige of the works of Chaucer and his contemporaries. . . .

Fortunately, it is far easier to read a language than to speak it. To get pleasure from reading Chaucer, it is not necessary to know Middle English grammar in detail; this short sketch of the language before Chaucer is intended merely to give the reader enough background to enable him to put Chaucer's English into perspective.

One thing to watch for, however, is the way in which many words have so changed in meaning since Chaucer's day while keeping much the same form: *nice* has already been instanced; *humour* is another outstanding one. The beginner must look up all words . . . at first, just in case they have changed in meaning. After a time he will learn the old meanings, and Chaucer will have on him something of the effect he intended 600 years ago. . . .

PRONUNCIATION

Chaucer's works were originally read aloud to an audience, not silently by individuals. A manuscript of *Troilus and Criseyde* in Trinity College, Cambridge, has as a frontispiece a picture of Chaucer reading to the Court. If we can learn to read him in an approximation to the original sound, much of his artistry will come clearer, and at the same time the meaning of many words which has been obscured by the spelling will be revealed by the relationship of the pronunciation to the modern sound. A rough and ready rule is to pronounce words of French origin as if they were French, and words of native or Germanic origin as if they were German. This works because the pronunciation of long vowels has, since Chaucer's day, changed far more in English than in continental languages. . . .

One of the trickiest problems in Chaucer pronunciation is that presented by the final –*e*, found at the end of many words. At the beginning of the 14th century these were generally sounded as separate syllables, but by the end of that century they had become silent, at any rate in common speech. Verse tends to retain the old-fashioned usages; final –*e* is still pronounced, or at least scanned, in French verse, centuries after it became silent in prose; and people's habits of speech do not change much as they grow older—which is why old people tend to sound old-fashioned and to criticize the speech-habits of their grandchildren which foreshadow what will become standard usage in another fifty years. On both these counts it looks as if we ought to pronounce the final –*e* except perhaps where it can be elided before a following vowel or silent *h.* Unfortunately, we cannot check this assumption by trying to scan Chaucer's verse, because theories about his versification [transformation of prose into verse] have been derived from presuppositions about his use of final –*e.* We are caught, in fact, in a circular argument.

THE RHYTHM OF THE LINES

From the 16th to the 19th centuries, as [Gerard Manley Hopkins,] one of the greatest technicians in verse, said, English verse has been

> measured by feet of either two or three syllables and (putting aside the imperfect feet at the beginning and end of lines and also some unusual measures, in which feet seem to be paired together and double or composite feet arise) never more nor less.

> Every foot has one principal stress or accent, and this or the syllable it falls on may be called the Stress of the foot and the other part, the one or two unaccented syllables, the Slack. Feet (and the rhythms made out of them) in which the Stress comes first are called Falling Feet and Falling Rhythms, feet and rhythm in which the Slack comes first are called Rising Feet and Rhythms, and if the Stress is between two Slacks there will be Rocking Feet and Rhythms.

But to prevent this basic rhythm from becoming monotonous, poets have always 'brought in licences and departures from the rule to give variety'. It is this 'Common English Rhythm', as Hopkins calls it, that unites the 18th-century heroic couplet and Shakespeare in a single tradition. . . .

Chaucer's verse, too, has usually been interpreted in the light of this tradition, so that the longer lines of his later work are read as five-stressed decasyllabic lines, and the shorter lines of his earlier work as four-stressed octosyl-labic. In each case the rhythm is rising—or iambic, to adopt the classical terminology. To ensure that Chaucer's verse fits this pattern, he is allowed by way of licence to have an extra unstressed syllable at the mid-line pause, or caesura, and at the end of the line, and to omit an unstressed initial sylla-ble—that is, to have only nine syllables in some lines. Unac-cented final –*e* must then be everywhere pronounced, ex-cept when it is followed by a vowel [or] a silent *h*. . . . Read on these assumptions, the first lines of the *Prologue* would go something like this:

```
    /   ×  / ×   \   ×  /  ×  / ×
Whan that Aprill with his shoures soote   (initial syllable omitted)

   ×    /     ×    /    ×   / ×  \ ×  / ×
The droght(e) of March hath perced to the roote,   (to stressed)

   ×  / ×  /×× /    ×   /    × /
And bathed every veyn(e) in swich licour

  ×    /   × /  ×  /  ×  \  ×    /
Of which vertu engendred is the flour:   (is stressed)

    ×   /  × /   ×   \   ×  /  ×   /
Whan Zephyrus eek with his sweete breeth   (with stressed)

  × / ×   /   × /×× /    ×    /
Inspired hath in every holt and heeth

   ×  /  ×  /  ×   \   ×  / ×  / ×
The tendre croppes, and the yonge sonne   (and stressed)

   /   × ×  /    ×  / ×  /   × / ×
Hath in the Ram his halve cours yronne,   (reversed first foot)

  ×  /  × /×× /   ×  /  × /×
And smale foweles maken melodye,   (extra syllable at caesura)

  ×    / × / × /    ×  /× /×
That slepen al the nyght with open ye

  ×  / ×   \    ×/   ×  \  × / ×
(So priketh hem Natur(e) in hir corages):   (hem, hir stressed)

     ×      /  × /  ×  /  × / ×/ ×
Thann(e) longen folk to goon on pilgrimages,

  ×  /   × ×  \ × / ×    /   ×  /   ×
And palmeres for to seken straunge strondes   (for stressed)
```

```
×  /  ×  /  ×   /    ×  /   ×  /  ×
```
To ferne halwes, kowth(e) in sondry londes;

Now theories of English grammar have, until comparatively recently, treated the language as if it were classical Latin. . . . Classical Latin verse consists of a pattern of long and short syllables arranged in a limited number of feet. A certain amount of substitution is permitted to prevent monotony, so that the number of syllables in a line may vary, though the number of feet is fixed. . . . This is the origin, not only of 'Common English Rhythm', but also of French and other modern European verse forms, which depend on a fixed number of syllables and pattern of stress.

OLD ENGLISH RHYTHMS

In view of this common origin there would have been no question about the sort of verse Chaucer wrote, were it not that Old English verse was constructed on very different principles, and this verse-form survived into Chaucer's lifetime. The Old English line was divided into two half-lines; each of these had two stressed syllables, and any convenient number of unstressed syllables, with, in some cases, a third lighter stress as well. There was no intentional rhyme. . . .

Now a recent attempt has been made to prove that Chaucer was in fact following this tradition in his verse, rather than the continental rhyming tradition of fixed numbers of syllables. J.G. Southworth, in *Verses of Cadence*, scans the opening lines of the *Prologue* somewhat like this:

```
  /   ×  /  ×  ×  ×    / ×  /
```
Whan that Aprill with his shoures soote

```
×   /    ×  /    ×   / × × ×  /
```
The droghte of March hath perced to the roote

```
×  /  ×  / ×   /   ×  /   × /
```
And bathed every veyne in swich licour

```
/  ×    / × × /  ×  /  ×  /
```
Of which vertu engendred is the flour

```
  /   /  × ×  /   ×   /    /   /
```
Whan Zephyrus eek with his sweete breeth

```
×  / ×  /   ×  / ×  /   ×  /
```
Inspired hath in every holt and heeth

```
×  /   ×  /   ×   × ×  /   /
```
The tendre croppes, and the yonge sonne

```
  /   × ×  /   ×  /   /  × /
```
Hath in the Ram his half cours yronne

```
 ×   /     / ×   /  × /  × /
And smale foweles maken melodye

  ×   / × / × /     ×   / × /
That slepen al the nyght with open ye

  ×  / ×  /    × /  ×  /  × / ×
(So priketh hem Nature in hir corages)

   /    / × /  ×  /   ×  / × / ×
Thanne longen folk to goon on pilgrimages

  ×  /  × × / × / ×    /      /   ×
And palmeres for to seken straunge strondes

  × /   / ×  /    × /   × / ×
To ferne halwes kowthe in sondry londes
```

The main difference between the two interpretations of this passage derives from the pronunciation or not of the final unstressed *-e.*

We do not know for certain whether Chaucer's contemporaries scanned it in the verse or not; we do think, however, that they did not pronounce it in normal speech

Southworth's contention is that all modern texts are edited on the assumption that the final *-e* was pronounced. ... A study of the manuscripts, he says, would support his opinion that the final *-e* was not scanned and that the verse is alliterative, not quantitative: native, that is, not continental. Since no extant [surviving] manuscript is in Chaucer's hand, and they are all written in the 15th century anyhow, there seems no likelihood of a definite solution as yet. Still, we can get the flavour of Chaucer's verse pretty well if we read him in the traditional way, remembering as we do it that behind the conventional iambic or rising rhythm there may be the older pattern of alliterative stressed verse, forming as it were a counterpoint.

CHAPTER 2

Important Themes in *The Canterbury Tales*

The Theme of Religious Pilgrimage in *The Canterbury Tales*

Esther C. Quinn

The fact that religious pilgrimage is an overriding theme of *The Canterbury Tales* at first glance seems too obvious to mention, since the overall setting of the work is a pilgrimage across the English country-side toward the shrine of Saint Thomas Becket at Canterbury cathedral. Yet, Chaucer goes far beyond this general use of the theme, lacing the *Tales* on many different levels with references to other pilgrimages, both ancient and contemporary. He also refers to various aspects and subthemes of religious journeys, including sacrifice, holy relics, penitence, martyrs, miracles, and redemption, to name only a few. In this essay, Esther C. Quinn, a noted scholar of medieval literature, discusses some of the major ways that Chaucer, by the clever introduction of fictional characters, imaginative situations, and key words, works and reworks the pilgrimage theme throughout the *Tales*.

The enormous and controversial subject of religion in the poetry of Chaucer might best be approached in a brief study by beginning with two generally accepted points: Chaucer was living in an age dominated by religious forces, and his poetry is permeated with religious references. Although the pervasive influence of religion on the poetry of Chaucer is widely recognized in numerous articles, notes in standard editions, and comments in book-length studies, there is no single comprehensive study of the subject. . . .

We shall approach the matter first by singling out from the complex world of fourteenth-century religion some of the elements that especially interested Chaucer; second by con-

From Esther C. Quinn, "Religion in Chaucer's *Canterbury Tales*: A Study in Language and Structure," in *Geoffrey Chaucer: A Collection of Original Articles*, edited by George D. Economou (New York: McGraw-Hill, 1975). Copyright 1975 by Esther C. Quinn. Reprinted by permission of the author.

sidering the relationship between religious language, which occurs throughout Chaucer's work, and religious structure, a somewhat more elusive concept; and finally by analyzing the way some of the religious elements appear as language and as structure in several of the *Canterbury Tales*, for it is on the pilgrimage to Canterbury that we can best trace the impact of fourteenth-century religion on Chaucer's poetry.

To a considerable extent, the religious language in Chaucer is a reflection of the dominating influence of the culture, which was, in externals at least, Christian. The frequency with which Chaucer's contemporaries referred to Christ, Mary, and the saints is echoed in his poetry, in the language of the pilgrims and in the tales they tell, especially those set in the Christian Era. But Chaucer is an artist and does not merely echo conventional pieties (or impieties); rather, as we shall see, he uses religious language in a variety of contexts, and it is only by considering the language in relation to the structure that we can arrive at his meaning.

Since religion played a significant role both in the real world of fourteenth-century England and in the world of Chaucer's poetry, we should consider first some of the aspects of the religion of his time that interested Chaucer and then explore, through an analysis of the religious language and structure, the way in which he transformed these real but transient aspects of the religion of his day into something fictitious but permanent.

TO WALK WHERE THE SAVIOR WALKED

Of the varied and complex world of fourteenth-century Christianity, certain aspects particularly interested Chaucer. A rough indication of his interests can be gauged by considering specific references, though ultimately the more accurate indication of his religious interests will be found in imaginative constructs rather than in the explicit use of religious language. A number of religious terms appear in a variety of contexts, which we might call key religious words. They not only recur throughout the text of the *Canterbury Tales* but also figure as structural units.

One of the most important of these key religious words, and the best one to begin with, is "pilgrimage." Pilgrimages were only one of the many aspects of fourteenth-century religious life to which Chaucer responded as a poet, but the fact that he made his *Canterbury Tales* one great pilgrimage suggests that the custom of pilgrimage became for him the concept of pilgrimage. In it are included all the elements of religion that interested him.

A pilgrimage was originally a spontaneous act of religious devotion, a journey to a distant holy site, a perilous undertaking involving hardship and sacrifice. The Christian practice of pilgrimage began in the early centuries following the death of Jesus and represented the desire of the faithful to walk upon the land where the Savior walked and thereby draw closer to his holy presence. By the third century, Christian pilgrims were making their way to the Holy Land. Over the centuries, the custom of making pilgrimages spread and pilgrimage sites multiplied, extending outward from Jerusalem and Bethlehem to Rome, Compostella, Cologne, and Bologna. By the fourteenth century, Canterbury had become England's most popular pilgrimage site, and Saint Thomas of Becket, England's greatest martyr-saint.

A great deal separates the sacrificial death of Jesus on Calvary and the murder of the archbishop in his cathedral at Canterbury. But they had this in common: the belief that a martyrdom had occurred, that the site of this martyrdom was sacred, and that to visit the site was to derive some of the material and spiritual benefits of the martyr's death.

What Chaucer knew or how he felt about the quarrel between Becket and his king which led to the archbishop's murder one can only speculate. But in the course of his *Canterbury Tales* Chaucer shows, besides his interest in the pilgrimage to Canterbury, a multitude of references to saints, martyrs, miracles, and relics.

By the fourteenth century, a pilgrimage for the most part was no longer an individual act of piety but rather a group undertaking in which religious motives play a part, yet the desire for companionship, pleasure, profit, or mere restlessness might figure more strongly. However great the contrast between the motley company that sets out from the Tabard Inn on that April morning and the archetypal act of devotion that led men to seek God at a particular site, the pilgrimage was still in Chaucer's day an essentially religious event, and reminders of this fact occur throughout the fictional pilgrimage.

A JOURNEY TOWARD THE SPIRITUAL

The opening movement of the *Canterbury Tales*, with its lovely description of an April morning, suggests the beginning of the world, when all things were fresh and new. April is a time to celebrate; April is full of promise. But as the poem progresses, the ways of fallen humanity intrude: drunkenness, quarreling, and swearing among the pilgrims, and in the tales they tell—cheating, vengeance, and murder.

BECKET'S MURDER AND MARTYRDOM

The story behind the Canterbury shrine is told in this excerpt from Life on a Medieval Pilgrimage, *by Don Nardo, who also cites scholar Gertrude Hartman's well-known book* Medieval Days and Ways.

Chaucer did not bother to explain to his readers why the pilgrims wanted to go to Canterbury. At the time, Canterbury cathedral housed the most famous and revered shrine in England and its contents and background were common knowledge. Everyone knew the story of King Henry II and his close friend and adviser Thomas Becket; how, in an attempt to check the growing power of the English bishops, in 1161 Henry made Becket archbishop of Canterbury, the highest religious post in the land; how, to Henry's surprise, Becket was so inspired by his new position that he renounced all luxury and put his duty to God before his duty to the king; and how four of Henry's knights, thinking they were doing the king a favor, murdered Becket in his own cathedral. In *Medieval Days and Ways*, scholar Gertrude Hartman explains why this act made Becket a holy martyr and inspired generations of pilgrims:

> To kill anyone within the sacred precincts of the church was an unspeakable crime, and the news of Becket's death filled all Europe with horror. The people feared that the curse of God would fall on a land where such a terrible thing had been done. Becket became a holy martyr of the church, and a magnificent shrine was built for him in the cathedral where he had lost his life. . . . It was a frequent sight in the spring of the year to see bands of pilgrims making their way to Canterbury to the martyr's shrine.

April may also be the Christian penitential season of Lent. Although in the beginning of the pilgrimage the sense of joyous anticipation is strong and there are few indications of the penitential possibility, references to Lent and to penance do crop up, and by the end the penitential aspect is sounded clearly. The words "penance" and "penitence," used in a number of contexts as the pilgrims make their way to Canterbury, serve as reminders of the penitential possibility, and the theme of penitence appears strongly at the end in the tale of the Parson, with his reminder that people will be forgiven if they will truly repent. The fictional pilgrimage rests upon the doctrines of the Fall and the Redemption; the structure of the *Canterbury Tales* parallels the Creation, Fall, and the promise of restoration to grace. There are other structures within the tales, but this is the structure of the pilgrimage.

By his use of the pilgrimage framework, Chaucer establishes the religious point of view from which we are to evaluate the characters, actions, and tales. Into the framework of a pilgrimage Chaucer has drawn a wide variety of religious elements from the Christian world of his own day. And the tale-telling scheme enables him, through fictional excursions into earlier times and distant places, to incorporate elements of paganism and primitive Christianity.

The pilgrimage toward Canterbury, though grounded in the reality of fourteenth-century English life by a multitude of specific references, is a conceptual pilgrimage. Chaucer moves from the actual custom of erring humans making pilgrimages into the idea of pilgrimage. In the Parson the actual and conceptual pilgrimages meet. To him the pilgrimage is an opportunity to join his sinful fellow pilgrims, to listen to them, and to urge them to repent. The pilgrimage is a metaphor for humanity's journey from a physical toward a spiritual reality. Few would claim that Chaucer's chief intent in writing the *Canterbury Tales* was either to express religious devotion or to point out the need for reform, but his choice of a pilgrimage as an organizing principle points to his acceptance of a religious dimension of reality that could be transformed into art. His use of the pilgrimage serves a number of purposes: it is a reminder of a religious environment, of religious values, and of a religious possibility.

ALL MEMBERS OF A CHRISTIAN COMMUNITY

The way Chaucer uses pilgrimage is typical of the way he uses a number of religious elements: he takes, in this instance, a religious custom and, by using the word in a number of contexts, creates both a concept of pilgrimage and a structure of pilgrimage. By examining the context in which actual references to pilgrimage occur, we can trace the interaction between the word "pilgrimage" and the structure of a pilgrimage. As we shall discover, Chaucer uses the device of pilgrimage to balance the possibility of religious devotion against the actuality of humanity's fallen state. References to pilgrimages and pilgrims occur not only in connection with the journey to Canterbury but in the tales the pilgrims tell and, more importantly, in the remarks of the Parson at the end. More significant than the references to the actual pilgrimage or even the metaphorical uses of the word is the pilgrimage as structure: the pilgrims moving from inn toward cathedral, from the Host's storytelling game to the Parson's treatise on penitence.

Although the pilgrimage is essentially a religious custom, the motives of individual pilgrims range from religious to irreligious. The primarily religious motivations might include seeking cures or favors or giving thanks for cures or favors received, assuaging a sense of guilt, or completing a penance imposed by one's confessor.

Although a pilgrimage might be undertaken for penitential reasons, there is little sense of this in the beginning of Chaucer's Canterbury pilgrimage. As the pilgrims start out from the Tabard Inn with the innkeeper as their self-proclaimed guide, having agreed to participate in his tale-telling game, the religious, especially the penitential, aspect of pilgrimage is minimized. It is easy to lose one's sense of the pilgrimage as a religious event because many of the pilgrims are such rascals: they drink to excess, swear, quarrel, deceive others and themselves; in short, they exhibit every form of vice and folly. And yet the sinful state of a considerable number of this heterogeneous [diverse] company should come as no surprise to anyone familiar with the doctrine of the Fall. Regardless of their behavior or motivation, they are Christians, fallen, in need of salvation. They are all members of a pilgrim community, united in being Canterbury-bound English Christians of the fourteenth century, the pilgrim-creations of Chaucer, brought into being by him to participate in his pilgrimage of pilgrimages.

The explicit purpose of the pilgrimage is religious, but the gathering of the pilgrims at the Tabard Inn, the physical point of departure, with all its associations of food, drink, lodging, and conviviality [sociability], establishes humanity's physical dimension. The pilgrims' easy acceptance of the innkeeper who proclaims himself their "governour," and their ready assent to his proposal that they engage in a tale-telling competition with the promise of a supper as the reward, serve as reminders of humanity's susceptibility to being led and misled. . . .

SOME PILGRIMS CONNECTED TO THE CHURCH

In his presentation of the pilgrims who are connected to the Church, Chaucer is interested both in the facade of holiness and in true holiness: in the Prioress, who mindlessly uses the trappings of holiness and in the Pardoner and Friar, who deliberately use the facade of holiness to deceive.

The six pilgrims who in the *General Prologue* are most closely connected with religion range from the vain Prioress, the defiant Monk, and wily Friar who is worldly and fleshly but affects a religious pose, the corrupt Summoner and the depraved Pardoner to the devout Parson. As the imperfections of the first five stem from their failures, misrepresentations, and abuses in relation to the institution of the Church, the goodness of the sixth and last is determined almost wholly in relation to the Gospel.

Besides these six religious pilgrims who are described in the *General Prologue,* there are two who accompany the Prioress—a nun and a priest. All eight tell tales. There is one other religious figure, a canon who joins the pilgrimage briefly and who exists chiefly in the tale his yeoman tells.

About one-third of the pilgrims have either taken religious vows or are associated with the organization of the Church. The other pilgrims making their way to Canterbury, although not deriving their livelihoods from the Church, are all Christian folk. The fact that they are on a pilgrimage serves as a reminder that they are products of a Christian society, exist in a religious context, and form part of a framework of religious values.

They are, however, not only a part of the religious framework, they exist in the immediate impact they have on the reader—and this emerges through the language that Chaucer the narrator uses and they themselves use, and this language is often explicitly Christian.

They are all pilgrims, the Wife of Bath, the Shipman, the Miller, and all the others. In the Miller, a pugilist [boxer], cheat and teller of ribald tales, Chaucer creates one of a number of instances of unredeemed humanity; to him, life—and the pilgrimage—is all pleasure and in no sense penitential. Like many another rascal, he is somewhat redeemed in the generous art of his creator by the brilliant tale he tells. As everyone knows, it is a bawdy story; what is perhaps less well known is that it is very rich in religious language. Although the uses to which this language is put are hardly devotional, the structure of the tale—the exposure and punishment of folly—is not inconsistent with a broadly conceived religious view.

THE CHARACTERS WITHIN THE TALES

There are in the *Canterbury Tales* two levels of characters: those whom Chaucer presents as fellow pilgrims and contemporaries and those who appear in the fictional world of the tales. Some of the stories the pilgrims tell reflect the fourteenth-century world, but quite often the fictional world extends to earlier times and distant places—pagan Greece, early Britain, ancient Rome. In some of the tales, the differentiation is almost complete; in others there are a juxtaposing and blending of Christian and pagan customs, terminology, values, and behavior. These excursions into fictional space and time provide Chaucer and his audience with a temporary and imaginative escape from their all-too "Christian" world with its bishops, sacraments, statues of the Virgin, crucifixes, and the like.

The characters in the tales range even more widely than the pilgrims: there are good pagans, that is, those who are placed in a pagan setting but who use language, respond to values, and exemplify ideals that are to some extent Christian; there are exemplary Christians, especially from earlier times; and there are pagans and Christians who are treacherous and murderous.

Some of the tales are set in England—where the characters seem virtually indistinguishable from the pilgrim characters. The difference is that these characters are caught up in a plot structure, as distinct from the pilgrimage structure, and although the language is Chaucer's, they are presented from the point of view of another pilgrim. For instance, the summoner in the *Friar's Tale* is virtually indistinguishable from the pilgrim-Summoner, but he is set in motion, put into a plot-structure, and given language by Chaucer's pilgrim-Friar. Similarly, the friar in the *Summoner's Tale.* . . .

The worst rascals among the "religious" pilgrims project the worst rascals in their tales: the wily Friar tells of a scoundrel-summoner; the rascally Summoner tells of an absurdly phony friar. The structure of the pilgrim-Friar's tale follows the pattern of vice-punished; it enables him to punish both the fictitious and pilgrim Summoner. And similarly the pilgrim-Summoner gets revenge on both the fictitious and the pilgrim-Friar. The self-centered and unscrupulous Pardoner follows up the exhibition of his fraudulent practices in his prologue with a tale that is an imaginative projection of deception, betrayal, and death in which three brothers-who-would-slay-death slay each other.

THE DIFFERENT KINDS OF TALES

A religious phenomenon of considerable interest is the sinner who repents. Although there are numerous references to repentance in the *Canterbury Tales* (in the tales of the Friar, Pardoner, and Parson, especially), there are no instances on the pilgrimage, and actual repentance is not even common in the fictional world of the tales.

A pattern closely related to the repentant sinner is religious conversion—in the explicitly religious tales, conversion from paganism to Christianity. The tales in which conversions take place—the Man of Law's and the Second Nun's—are interestingly enough set in earlier times. Conversion in the tales is a simple occurrence, a matter of statement. The actual process of change from sinfulness to holiness is not represented.

The characters in the tales—as well as the pilgrims—exist in a religious context ranging from the Christian (though irreligious) fourteenth century to the surprisingly Christian world of the pagan past. Thus, through the use of different cultural settings and the introduction of both exemplary and depraved characters, Chaucer explores a variety of value systems in the fictional world of his *Canterbury Tales*.

Among the explicitly Christian tales are those of the Prioress, the Second Nun, the Clerk, the Man of Law, Chaucer's own tale of Melibeus, and the final "tale" of the Canterbury pilgrimage, the Parson's treatise on penitence and the seven deadly sins.

There are other tales in which a great deal of explicitly Christian language is used, but the context is anything but religious. Here the structure may serve a religious purpose, but it functions differently from the straight Christian tales; instead of exemplifying virtue, these tales mock vice and folly and expose fraud and hence have a cleansing, purging effect. They may be humorous, even bawdy; they may be told in a spirit of mockery or even malice, but the structure serves a moral purpose and insofar as morality is a component of religion, they serve a religious purpose. Among these are the tales of the Friar and the Summoner and the *Nun's Priest's Tale.*

A third type of religious tale is, like the first group, serious, but like the second, aimed at the exposure of vice; the best example of this is the *Pardoner's Tale.*

Belonging to a special group are several tales that deal essentially with virtuous actions but are not explicitly Christian; they may, like the *Knight's Tale*, have pagan settings and pagan religious elements that are, however, similar to those in the Christian tales.

What remains are the fabliaux—the tales of the Miller, the Reeve, the Shipman, and the Merchant. Essentially entertainment, all involve sex and tricks. They too are permeated by religious references, for the most part explicitly Christian, but the effect of the religious language in inappropriate contexts is hilarious. . . .

A BLEND OF PAGAN AND CHRISTIAN

Throughout the *Canterbury Tales* Chaucer balances religious and profane elements: piety and impiety, reverence and irreverence, sincere religious devotion and the satirical use of religious forms. In varying combinations he juxtaposes and blends pagan and Christian language and values, contrasting and weighing possibilities and consequences. There are the limited good of the *Knight's Tale*, the ugly vision of the *Merchant's Tale*, the bright world of the *Franklin's Tale.*

The continuous use of religious references serves as a reminder that the pilgrimage is not merely a social or literary venture; these references function as reminders of the spiritual possibilities of pilgrimage. Chaucer moves toward the end of the *Canterbury Tales* closer to exclusively Christian concerns. In placing the *Parson's Tale* and his own *Retraction* last, he sets the whole work in a Christian perspective.

Chaucer is not primarily a religious poet, as Dante and Langland are. But he is a great and original poet whose viewpoint is essentially Christian. For many of his richest and most characteristic effects he uses religious language, and throughout the *Canterbury Tales* he uses religious structures—in the tales and in the pilgrimage itself. In the end, the language and the structures are Chaucer's.

Social Rank in
The Canterbury Tales

Donald R. Howard

As the respected Chaucerian scholar Donald R.
Howard points out in this excerpt from his book
Chaucer: His Life, His Works, His World, the General
Prologue of *The Canterbury Tales* is in large degree
an organizing device that helps unify and clarify the
various sections of the work. In the Prologue,
Howard explains, Chaucer presents the diverse characters in groups representing their ranks in the
social order of the day, which consisted of three or
four basic types of people. Howard also compares
Chaucer's ability at literary portraiture to the art of
medieval Italian portrait painting. In both, according
to this view, the artists captured all of their subjects'
qualities, including the bad ones, even when there
was a marked difference between the social ranks of
artists and subjects.

The General Prologue is the heart or backbone of *The Canterbury Tales.* It imposes in advance the "outer" structure of
the pilgrimage and the "inner" structure of the pilgrims' tales.
In introducing the pilgrims Chaucer arranged them so that
we can see their relationships and remember them more easily. The Knight rides with his son and a servant or retainer,
the Prioress with another nun and three priests, the London
Guildsmen with their wives and hired cook, the crooked Pardoner with his cohort the Summoner. The Sergeant of Law
and the Franklin, both great purchasers of land, ride together.
Others are described *as if* they rode together: Prioress, Monk,
and Friar; Clerk and Merchant; Manciple, Reeve, and Miller;
Shipman, Physician, and Wife. The Miller rides colorfully in
front, tooting his bagpipe; the Reeve, the Miller's enemy, and
a suspicious man by nature, rides last.

From *Chaucer: His Life, His Works, His World* by Donald R. Howard. Copyright ©1987
by the Estate of Donald R. Howard. Used by permission of Dutton Signet, a division of
Penguin Books USA Inc.

A DESCENDING SOCIAL ORDER

In this description Chaucer embedded an old-fashioned ideal of social harmony, "the Three Estates." It was thought society consisted of knights, clergy, and commons, "those who fight, those who pray, and those who work.". . . Chaucer . . . included an ideal member of each Estate: the Knight (described as a crusader), the Parson (a self-sacrificing parish priest), and his "brother" the Plowman (who "lived in peace and perfect charity"). The Clerk seems idealized too, though as a student he has not yet defined his place in adult life—he is described in terms of what he does not have or want, what he would like, and so on. The largest number of pilgrims are of the "commons," which reflects the social circumstances of the day: the commons were now stratified into intermediate classes extending up to the rich and powerful, like the Man of Law or the Franklin, and down to the poor and marginal, like the drunken Cook.

Chaucer arranged these groups in a sequence from high to low, divided symmetrically by the ideal portraits. First are the Knight and his small retinue, the Prioress and hers, and the Monk and Friar; next the Merchant, introducing members of the "middle" and merchant class; and last the "churls," introduced first in a lump (lines 542–544), among whom Chaucer wryly includes himself.

To this descending social order he coupled a descending order of morality. He at first hints so delicately at the pilgrims' transgressions that we are not sure we hear him right: some hear him say that the Knight is an ideal crusader, some that he belongs to a part of the knighthood that has ceased to scrutinize its values, some that he is a mercenary. The Knight's son is more a courtier than a soldier, whose one "crusade" has been the bishop of Norwich's disreputable "Glorious Campaign" of 1383—there is nothing necessarily wrong with him, but the institution he has been raised to has fallen in decay. The Prioress is charming and ladylike, perhaps ever so slightly pathetic, and we respond with human warmth to her elegant dress and manner, her little dogs, her gold jewelry, even while we are aware that these are small infringements against convent rules. The infringements of the Monk and Friar are lechery and avarice, the charges so often brought against them. We recognize medieval "estates satire" creeping into the descriptions. The Lawyer and Doctor use their positions for personal gain;

their transgressions are pretentiousness, ostentation, greed. The Shipman makes enemies walk the plank, the Wife of Bath has profited from marrying and outliving her numerous older husbands. The final group of "churls," the Miller, Reeve, and Manciple, possess the same greed and slipperiness but in smaller, meaner ways; at the end come the obnoxious Summoner and Pardoner, feeding upon the simple faith of ordinary people.

MEDIEVAL EUROPEAN SOCIAL CLASSES

In this excerpt from his book The Age of Faith, *historian Will Durant comments about social ranking in the Middle Ages.*

In the early Middle Ages there had been only two classes in western Europe: German conquerors and native conquered; by and large the later aristocracies in England, France, Germany and northern Italy were descendants of the conquerors, and remained conscious of this blood relationship even amid their wars. In the eleventh century there were three classes: the nobles, who fought; the clergy, who prayed; and the peasants, who worked. The division became so traditional that most men thought it ordained by God; and most peasants, like most nobles, assumed that a man should patiently continue in the class into which he had been born.

The economic revolution of the twelfth century added a new class—the burgesses or *bourgeoisie*—the bakers, merchants, and master craftsmen of the towns. It did not yet include the professions. In France the classes were called *états*—estates or states—and the *bourgeoisie* was reckoned as the *tiers état*, or "third estate." It controlled municipal affairs, and [eventually] won entry into the English Parliament, the German Diet, the Spanish Cortes, and the States-General—the rarely convened national parliament of France; but it had, before the eighteenth century, little influence on national policy. The nobles continued to rule and administer the state, though they were now a minor force in the cities. They lived in the country (except in Italy), scorned city dwellers and commerce, ostracized any of their class who married a bourgeois, and were certain that an aristocracy of birth is the only alternative to a plutocracy of business, or a theocracy of myths.

The narrator remains throughout a credulous bourgeois [middle-class person] of unflagging enthusiasm who admires cleverness and success, even successful thievery, and empathizes with the social climbers and the snobs. Saint Augustine had said Christians must "hate the sin but love the sinner"; the narrator's attitude is like a comic, slightly grotesque charade of this principle—he fails to make the necessary distinction and seems to love their vices too! Beneath the pose of the *naïf* we are aware of the poet himself using the device to satirize his countrymen, but he still makes God's love shine reflected in the narrator's simple-mindedness.

RANK, DRESS, AND NAME

The General Prologue seems an original feat of literary ingenuity, but in composing it Chaucer used the form of the dream vision. . . . The Prologue *is* dreamlike: at first we seem to be in the Tabard Inn, but we are not, for the pilgrims are described as they ride together along the way. Yet we are not along the way either, for we learn intimate details about the pilgrims' domestic circumstances, their histories, even their private thoughts. We watch the Prioress feeding her dogs in her convent, we observe the Monk's horses and stables, we savor the Pardoner's expectancy before he rises to preach. We are in the narrator's memory of what he had seen and heard, what people told him, what he guessed or surmised or imagined. He is not an "omniscient" narrator: he tells us what he doesn't know, for example the Merchant's name (though he knows the Friar's), tells us only as much as he saw, for example the Prioress's puzzling brooch, and tells us things sometimes in ambiguous language. . . .

And this dreamlike quality of the General Prologue is part of its "realism"—for realism is artifice too. The conventional way to describe a person in medieval rhetoric started with the head and proceeded downward, but Chaucer abandoned the convention in favor of his "impressionism." He tells us he will report about each pilgrim what is "accordant to reason". . . the circumstances of each as it seemed to him, which was which, what their rank was, and how they were dressed. He gives us details as one remembers them, helter-skelter and in fragments, by first impressions and associations. The Squire is first described as a "lover and a lusty bachelor," with curly locks, twenty years old; he has been on "chivachie" in Flanders, Artois, and Picardy, which would have been recognized as the scandalous "crusade" led by the bishop of Norwich, now wryly known as "The Glorious Campaign." He wears an embroidered garment, sings all day, wears a fashionable short tunic with long sleeves, can sit a horse and ride, and compose songs—the organization is selective, associative.

The narrator doesn't hesitate to generalize or comment. He says the Prioress is charitable and compassionate, is at pains to emulate the manner of the court, be dignified in her comportment, be held worthy of reverence. Certain details are so specific and unexplained that they have almost a sacramental quality. The Prioress's brooch, of gold, with its crowned *A* and its motto *amor vincit omnia,* is some kind of keepsake, elegant, expensive, probably secular, but ambiguous enough that we can believe *she* believed it was religious.

We know the pilgrims largely by such signs, presented as shared culture traits. For example their names, of which we know only a few, can be subtly characterizing: Eglantine was an elegant name, Alisoun a name (in contemporary songs) for country wenches, Robin and Oswald low-class names. So with clothes: Chaucer understood that clothes are a language designating social status, attitude, psychological fix. "Fashion," as was said earlier, was new in Chaucer's time; it had come a generation or two before, with the invention of tailoring, which encouraged shaping the body into created "looks." The Squire's short embroidered gown with long sleeves identifies a courtly fashion and distinguishes him from his father, who is dressed for battle. The Prioress's wimple is pushed back, against convent rules, to reveal her ample forehead, a sign of beauty. The Monk's furs and gold pin with its "love-knot" show he is an aristocrat, a lusty one who we are told "loved venerie." The way they wear their hair (the Reeve's is shorn round about his ears) and the horses they ride help place them in social ranks. We do not very much, in the General Prologue, see into their minds.

LIKE PAINTED PORTRAITS

In *The Canterbury Tales* Chaucer developed an effect in literary portraiture rather like one that was to emerge in Italian portrait painting in the next century. It is hard to be certain what was the provenance of this effect, for which there is apparently no name. It involves his actual presence in the work as the artist, as opposed to the narrator or persona he uses as a mask. This effect is seen dramatically in the paintings often called *Portrait of a Young Man*, a genre of Renaissance art. In them the artist was commissioned to paint the young son of a patron, and it evidently became a tradition for him to paint what he saw, a spoiled aristocrat not yet capable of concealing adolescent emotions. The young subject appears impatient at sitting still for the artist, and looks at him as at a social inferior. We see him through the artist's eyes and then see the artist himself reflected in his facial expression: it is a portrait of an interaction. The painters could have made their subjects smile or show blossoming manhood, innate generosity, nobility of character, but no: they painted them as they experienced them, aloof, preoccupied, self-absorbed. We feel or sense the artist's slight annoyance and perhaps—as never in the young man—his amusement.

Chaucer attains this effect mostly by what he refrains from telling. We are left to puzzle with him over the Prioress's brooch; we can see that she is from a good family but not so good that "chiere of court" [courtly manners] is natural to her nor so well traveled that she speaks other than déclassé Anglo-French. . . . Her mysterious medallion *means* something, and part of what it means is that the author himself has taken special note of it and chooses to hold his tongue about it. We learn about the pilgrims from the naïve narrator and hear his views about them, but we see them through the interacting, discerning, skeptical eye of the poet himself.

With many of the pilgrims the portraits in the General Prologue raise questions: we feel there is more here than meets the eye, we approach their tales on the lookout for something revealing in their choice of subject, or in their characters, the story itself, or the manner of its telling. To be sure some tales offer few surprises and some portraits don't raise questions. The Merchant, as first described, is typical; but then Chaucer added in the prologue to his tale a fact that accounts for his bitter antifeminist story—he has been married two months and has already found his wife a shrew.

THE ELEMENT OF MYSTERY

Chaucer saw, as apparently [his contemporary, the Italian poet Giovanni] Boccaccio did not, that the tale each told could tell a tale about its teller. It is the pilgrims' tales that make us think we know them. What if the Knight had told the tale of the patient Griselda . . . which the Clerk tells, and the Clerk had told the Knight's epic of classical times adapted from Boccaccio? What if the Wife had told the cynical tale the Shipman tells (there is some evidence Chaucer first assigned that tale to her), or if the Prioress or Monk had told the life of Saint Cecile, the one true saint's legend, told by the Second Nun? Some critics downplay Chaucer's use of the tales to characterize the tellers, but he grasped the principle: the Wife's Tale evokes her inner wishes as perfectly as if it were a dream, shows us something about her we couldn't have known otherwise. All agree that the Knight's Tale is appropriate to the Knight, the Miller's to the Miller, and so on. But some tales make us see or suspect qualities not yet revealed, like the Prioress's cruel story about the "wicked Jews" or the Monk's stuffy collection of tragic stories about the downfalls of the great. These tales that seem to provide a deeper insight into their tellers bring us, however, into the realm of contradictions or inconsistencies in character, which is itself mysterious. The realism of *The Canterbury Tales* lies not in the "photographic" details but in this element of mystery. We are in a society whose rules [of social ranking] we know and about whose small details we feel we can make informed guesses, a milieu of the greatest particularity—where, as in the world about us, particulars may jar or puzzle.

The Theme of Marriage in *The Canterbury Tales*

G.L. Kittredge

The tales told by the pilgrims on their way to Canterbury in Chaucer's famous work are not simply a sequence of unrelated stories; rather, the themes and ideas of one tale often develop directly from those of a preceding tale. Indeed, sometimes a pilgrim takes exception to a fellow traveler's view on a subject and proceeds to tell his or her own story as a sort of reaction or rebuttal to that view. This use of overriding and recurring themes ties together the diverse stories and characters into the larger framework we know as *The Canterbury Tales*. In the following essay, one of the most famous ever written about the *Tales*, the renowned and highly respected Chaucerian scholar G.L. Kittredge discusses the so-called Marriage Group, a sequence of tales relating to the subject of marriage, all of which, he contends, are sparked by the outspoken comments of the lusty Wife of Bath.

We are prone to read and study the *Canterbury Tales* as if each tale were an isolated unit and to pay scant attention to what we call the connecting links,—those bits of lively narrative and dialogue that bind the whole together. Yet Chaucer's plan is clear enough. Structurally regarded, the *Canterbury Tales* is a kind of Human Comedy. From this point of view, the Pilgrims are the *dramatis personae* [characters of this comic play], and their stories ... in each case ... illustrate the speaker's character and opinions, or show the relations of the travelers to one another in the progressive action of the Pilgrimage. In other words, we ought not merely to consider the general appropriateness of each tale to the character of the teller: we should also inquire whether the tale is not determined, to some extent, by the circum-

From G.L. Kittredge, "Chaucer's Discussion of Marriage," *Modern Philology*, vol. 9, (1912), pp. 435-67.

stances,—by the situation at the moment, by something that another Pilgrim has said or done, by the turn of a discussion already under way.

Now and then, to be sure, this point is too obvious to be overlooked, as in the squabble between the Summoner and the Friar and that between the Reeve and the Miller, in the Shipman's intervening to check the Parson, and in the way in which the gentles head off the Pardoner when he is about to tell a ribald anecdote [dirty story]. But, despite these unescapable instances, the general principle is too often blinked or ignored. . . .

FORTITUDE IN ADVERSITY

Without attempting to deny or abridge the right to study and criticize each tale in and for itself . . . let us consider certain tales in their relation to Chaucer's structural plan,—with reference, that is to say, to the Pilgrims who tell them and to the Pilgrimage to which their telling is incidental. We may begin with the story of Griselda.

This is a plain and straightforward piece of edification, and nobody has ever questioned its appropriateness to the Clerk, who, as he says himself, had traveled in Italy and had heard it from the lips of the laureate Petrarch [a fourteenth-century Italian poet]. The Clerk's "speech," according to the General Prologue, was "sowning in moral vertu," so that this story is precisely the kind of thing which we should expect from his lips. True, we moderns sometimes feel shocked or offended at what we style the immorality of Griselda's unvarying submission [to her husband, who repeatedly tested her love and devotion to him by demanding that she give up custody of her children without the slightest objection]. But this feeling is no ground of objection to the appropriateness of the tale to the Clerk. The Middle Ages delighted (as children still delight) in stories that exemplify a single human quality, like valor, or tyranny, or fortitude. In such cases, the settled rule . . . was to show to what lengths this quality may conceivably go. Hence, in tales of this kind, there can be no question of conflict of duties, no problem as to the point at which excess of goodness becomes evil. . . . Whether Griselda could have put an end to her woes, or ought to have put an end to them, by refusing to obey her husband's commands is *parum ad rem* [beside the point]. We are to look at her trials as inevitable, and to pity her accordingly, and wonder at her endurance. If we refuse to accept the tale in this spirit, we are ourselves the losers. We miss the pathos because we are aridly intent on discussing an ethical question that has no status in this particular court, however pertinent it may be in the general forum of morals.

Furthermore, in thus focusing attention on the morality or immorality of Griselda's submissiveness, we overlook what the Clerk takes pains to make as clear as possible,—the real lesson that the story is meant to convey,—and thus we do grave injustice to that austere but amiable moralist. . . .

IS HAVING FIVE HUSBANDS A SIN?

The Wife of Bath's bold, unapologetic, and unrepentant attitude toward marriage is illustrated in this excerpt from Barbara Cohen's prose version of the prologue to her famous tale.

"If there were no authorities in this world," she said, "experience alone gives me the right to talk about the trouble that is in marriage. Thanks to the eternal God, I've been married five times, and all my husbands were respectable men. Not long ago someone told me that since Christ went to only one wedding, in Cana of Galilee, I should have married only once. But I know that God commanded us to be fruitful and multiply. He also said a man should leave his father and mother and cleave to his wife. But He didn't mention any number, so why should people consider five marriages a sin?

"Look at wise King Solomon: I believe he had more than one wife. Thank God I've married five men. The sixth will be welcome whenever he comes. To tell the truth, I won't stay single when my husband is gone from this world. Some Christian man will marry me soon enough. St. Paul said it's better to marry than to burn. Abraham and Jacob were holy men, and each of them had more than two wives. Can you show me any place where God forbade marriage in so many words? Men may advise women to stay single, but advice isn't a commandment."

Chaucer had too firm a grasp on his *dramatis personae* to allow the Clerk to leave the true purport of his parable undefined. "This story is not told," says the Clerk in substance, "to exhort wives to imitate Griselda's humility, for *that* would be beyond the capacity of human nature. It is told in order that every man or woman, in whatever condition of life, may learn fortitude in adversity. For, since a woman once exhibited such endurance under trials inflicted on her by a mortal man ... ought *we* to accept patiently whatever tribulation God may send us. For God is not like Griselda's husband. He does not wantonly experiment with us, out of inhuman scientific curiosity. God *tests* us, as it is reasonable that our Maker should test his handiwork, but he does not *tempt* us.". ...

WIVES SHOULD RULE THEIR HUSBANDS

And then, at verse 1163, comes that matchless passage in which the Clerk ... turns with gravely satiric courtesy to the Wife of Bath and makes the *particular* application of the story to her "life" and "all her sect."

Here one may appreciate the vital importance of considering the *Canterbury Tales* as a connected Human Comedy,— of taking into account the Pilgrims in their relations to one another in the great drama to which the several narratives are structurally incidental. ...

[Why did] the Clerk, after emphasizing the serious and universal moral of Griselda's story ... [pay] tribute to the Wife of Bath, her life, her "sect," and her principles? To answer this question we must go back to the Wife of Bath's Prologue.

The Wife of Bath's Prologue begins a Group in the *Canterbury Tales*, or, as one may say, a new act in the drama. It is not connected with anything that precedes. Let us trace the action from this point down to the moment when the Clerk turns upon the Wife with his satirical compliments.

The Wife had expounded her views at great length and with all imaginable zest. Virginity, which the Church glorifies, is not required of us. Our bodies are given us to use [for sex]. Let saints be continent if they will. She has no wish to emulate them. Nor does she accept the doctrine that a widow or a widower must not marry again. Where is bigamy forbidden in the Bible, or octogamy either? She has warmed both hands before the fire of life, and she exults in the recollection of her fleshly delights. ... True, she is willing to admit, for convention's sake, that chastity is the ideal state. But it is not *her* ideal. On the contrary, her admission is only for appearances. In her heart she despises virginity. Her contempt for it is thinly veiled, or rather, not veiled at all. ... Her whole attitude is that of scornful, though good-humored, repudiation of what the Church teaches in that regard.

Nor is the Wife content with this single heresy. She maintains also that wives should rule their husbands, and she enforces this doctrine by an account of her own life. . . .

Now the Wife of Bath . . . addresses her heresies not to *us* or to the world at large, but to her fellow-pilgrims. Chaucer has made this point perfectly clear. The words of the Wife were of a kind to provoke comment,—and we have the comment. The Pardoner interrupts her with praise of her noble preaching. . . . It is manifest, then, that Chaucer meant us to imagine the *dramatis personae* as taking a lively interest in whatever the Wife says. This being so, we ought to inquire what effect her Prologue and Tale would have upon the Clerk.

Of course the Clerk was scandalized. He was unworldly. . . . Moral virtue was his special study. He had embraced the celibate life. He was grave, devout, and unflinchingly orthodox. And now he was confronted by the lust of the flesh and the pride of life in the person of a woman who flouted chastity and exulted that she had "had her world as in her time." Nor was this all. The woman . . . set up, and aimed to establish, a new and dangerous sect, whose principle was that the wife should rule the husband. The Clerk kept silence for the moment. . . . But it is not to be imagined that his thoughts were idle. He could be trusted to speak to the purpose whenever his opportunity should come. . . .

THE WIFE TELLS HER STORY

Chaucer might have given the Clerk a chance to reply to the wife immediately. But he was too good an artist. The drama of the Pilgrimage is too natural and unforced in its development. . . . The Pilgrims were interested in the Wife's harangue, but it was for the talkative members of the company to thrust themselves forward. The Pardoner had already interrupted her with humorous comments before she was fully under way and had exhorted [urged] her to continue her account of . . . marriage. The Friar we may be confident was on good terms with her before she began. . . . He, too, could not refrain from comment. . . . The Summoner reproved him, in words that show not only his professional enmity but also the amusement that the Pilgrims in general were deriving from the Wife's disclosures. They quarreled, and each threatened to tell a story at the other's expense. Then the Host intervened roughly, calling for silence and bidding the Wife go ahead with her story. . . .

The quarrel between the Summoner and the Friar was in

abeyance [postponed] until the Wife finished her tale. They let her end her story and proclaim her moral in peace,—the same heretical doctrine that we have already noted, that the wife should be the head of the house. . . .

Then follows the comic interlude of the Friar and the Summoner, in the course of which we may perhaps lose sight of the serious subject which the Wife had set abroach,—the status of husband and wife in the marriage relation. But Chaucer did not lose sight of it. It was a part of his design that the Host should call on the Clerk for the first story of the next day.

The Clerk's Retort to the Wife of Bath

This is the opportunity for which the Clerk has been waiting. He has not said a word in reply to the Wife's heresies or to her personal attack on him and his order. Seemingly she has triumphed. The subject has apparently been dismissed with the Friar's words about leaving such matters to sermons and to school debates. The Host, indeed, has no idea that the Clerk purposes to revive the discussion. . . .

"Tell us a tale," the unconscious Host goes on, "but don't preach us a Lenten sermon—tell us som mery thing of aventures." "Gladly," replies the demure scholar. "I will tell you a story that a *worthy* clerk once told me at Padua—Francis Petrarch, God rest his soul!"

At this word *clerk*, pronounced with grave and inscrutable emphasis, the Wife of Bath must have pricked up her ears. But she has no inkling of what is in store, nor is the Clerk in any hurry to enlighten her. He opens with tantalizing deliberation, and it is not until he has spoken more than sixty lines that he mentions marriage. "The Marquis Walter," says the Clerk, "lived only for the present and lived for pleasure only.". . .

Clearly the Clerk is catching up the subject proposed by the Wife. The discussion is under way again.

Yet, despite the cheerful view that Walter's subjects take of the marriage yoke, it is by no means yet clear to the Wife of Bath and the other Pilgrims what the Clerk is driving at. For he soon makes Walter declare that "liberty is seldom found in marriage," and that, if he weds a wife, he must exchange freedom for servitude. Indeed, it is not until [several lines later] that Walter reveals himself as a man who is determined to rule his wife absolutely. From that point to the end there is no room for doubt in any Pilgrim's mind: *the Clerk is answering the Wife of Bath*; he is telling of a woman whose principles in marriage were the antithesis [complete opposite] of hers; he is reasserting the orthodox view in opposition to the heresy which she had expounded with such zest and with so many flings and jeers at the clerkly profession and character.

What is the tale of Griselda? . . . Our present concern . . . is primarily with the question what it seemed to be to the Canterbury Pilgrims, told as it was by an individual Clerk of Oxford at a particular moment and under the special circumstances. The answer is plain. To them it was a retort (indirect, impersonal, masterly) to the Wife of Bath's heretical [irreligious] doctrine that the woman should be the head of the man. It told them of a wife who had no such views,—who promised ungrudging obedience and kept her vow. The Wife of Bath had railed at her husbands and badgered them and cajoled them: Griselda never lost her patience or her serenity. On its face, then, the tale appeared to the Pilgrims to be a dignified and scholarly narrative, derived from a great Italian clerk who was dead, and now utilized by their fellow-pilgrim, the Clerk of Oxford, to demolish the heretical structure so boisterously reared by the Wife of Bath in her prologue and her tale. . . .

The Clerk has no idea of failing to make his point against the Wife of Bath. And so, when the tale is finished and the proper Petrarchan moral has been duly elaborated, he turns to the Wife (whom he has thus far sedulously refrained from addressing) and distinctly applies the material to the purpose of an ironical answer, of crushing force, to her whole heresy. There is nothing inappropriate to his character in this procedure. Quite the contrary. Clerks were always satirizing women—the Wife had said so herself—and this particular Clerk had, of course, no scruples against using the powerful weapon of irony in the service of religion. . . . In this instance, the satire is peculiarly poignant for two reasons: first, because it comes with all the suddenness of a complete change of tone (from high seriousness to biting irony, and from the impersonal to the personal); and secondly, because, in the tale which he has told, the Clerk has incidentally refuted a false statement of the Wife's. . . .

THE MERCHANT'S HEARTFELT STORY

And then comes the Clerk's Envoy, the song that he recites in honor of the Wife and her life and her sect, with its polished lines, its ingenious rhyming, and its utter felicity of scholarly diction. Nothing could be more in character. To whom in all the world should such a masterpiece of rhetoric be appropriate if not to the Clerk of Oxenford? It is a mock encomium [tribute], a sustained ironical commendation of what the Wife has taught:

"O noble wives, let no clerk ever have occasion to write such a story of you as Petrarch once told me about Griselda. Follow your great leader, the Wife of Bath. Rule your husbands, as she did; rail at them, as she did; make them jealous, as she did; exert yourselves to get lovers, as she did. And all this you must do whether you are fair or foul. . . . Do this, I say, and you will fulfil the precepts that she has set forth and achieve the great end which she has proclaimed as the object of marriage: that is, *you will make your husbands miserable, as she did!*". . .

The Clerk's Envoy, then, is not only appropriate to his character and to the situation: it has also a marked dynamic value. For it is this ironical tribute to the Wife of Bath and her dogmas that, with complete dramatic inevitability, calls out the Merchant's [heartfelt story]. The Merchant has no thought of telling a tale at this moment. He is a stately and imposing person in his degree, by no means prone (so the Prologue informs us) to expose any holes there may be in his coat. But he is suffering a kind of emotional crisis. The poignant irony of the Clerk, following hard upon the moving story of a patient and devoted wife, is too much for him. He has just passed through his honeymoon (but two months wed!) and he has sought a respite from his thraldom [bondage, for he sees his new wife as cruel and overbearing] under color of a pilgrimage to St. Thomas. . . . The Host, as ever, is on the alert. He scents a good story. . . . The Merchant agrees, as in duty bound, for all the Pilgrims take care never to oppose the Host, lest he exact the heavy forfeit established as the penalty for rebellion. But he declines to relate his own experiences, thus leaving us to infer, if we choose . . . that his bride has proved false to him. . . .

And so the discussion of marriage is once more in full swing. The Wife of Bath, without intending it, has opened a debate in which the Pilgrims have become so absorbed that they will not leave it till the subject is "bolted to the bran.". . .

[Indeed, the] end of the Merchant's Tale does not bring the Marriage Chapter of the *Canterbury Tales* to a conclusion. As the Merchant had commented on the Clerk's Tale by speaking of his own wife, thus continuing the subject which the Wife had begun, so the Host comments on the Merchant's story by making a similar application: "See how women deceive us poor men, as the Merchant has shown us. However, *my* wife is true as any steel; but she is a shrew, and has plenty of other faults." And just as the Merchant had referred expressly to the Wife of Bath, so also does the Host refer to her expressly: "But I must not talk of these things. If I should, it would be told to her by some of this company. I need not say by whom.". . . Of course the Host points this remark by looking at the Wife of Bath. . . . And so we find the Wife of Bath still in the foreground, as she has been, in one way or another, for several thousand lines. . . .

A SATISFACTORY CONCLUSION OF THE MARRIAGE

But Chaucer's plan in this Act is not yet finished. There is still something lacking to a full discussion of the relations between husband and wife. We have had the wife who dominates her husband; the husband who dominates his wife; the young wife who befools her dotard January; the chaste wife who is a scold and stirs up strife. Each of these illustrates a different kind of marriage,—but there is left untouched, so far, the ideal relation, that in which love continues and neither party to the contract strives for the mastery. Let this be set forth, and the series of views of wedded life begun by the Wife of Bath will be rounded off; the Marriage Act of the Human Comedy will be concluded. The Pilgrims may not be thinking of this; but there is at least *one* of them (as the sequel shows) who has the idea in his head. And who is he? The only pilgrims who have not already told their tales are the yeoman, two priests, the five tradesmen (haberdasher, carpenter, weaver, dyer, and tapicer), the parson, the plowman, the manciple, and the franklin. Of all these there is but one to whom a tale illustrating this ideal would not be inappropriate—the Franklin. To him, then, must Chaucer assign it, or leave the debate unfinished. . . .

The introductory part of the Franklin's Tale sets forth a theory of the marriage relation quite different from anything that has so far emerged in the debate. And this theory the Franklin arrives at by taking into consideration both *love* . . . and *gentillesse* [the quality of gentleness and good breeding; his story concerns a knight and his young wife who are very much in love; a young squire also loves her; each man, out of love for her and also out of a noble spirit of chivalry, reluctantly offers to give her up to the other; eventually, she ends up with her husband]. . . .

It was the regular theory of the Middle Ages that the highest type of chivalric love was incompatible with marriage, since marriage brings in mastery, and mastery and love cannot abide together. This view the Franklin boldly challenges. Love *can* be consistent with marriage, he declares. Indeed, without love (and perfect, *gentle* love) marriage is sure to be a failure. The difficulty about mastery vanishes when mutual love and forbearance are made the guiding principles of the relation between husband and wife.

The soundness of the Franklin's theory, he declares, is proved by his tale. For the marriage of Arveragus and Dorigen [the husband and wife in his story] was a brilliant success. . . . Thus the whole debate has been brought to a satisfactory conclusion, and the Marriage Act of the Human Comedy ends with the conclusion of the Franklin's Tale.

Those readers who are eager to know what Chaucer thought about marriage may feel reasonably content with the inference that may be drawn from his procedure. The Marriage Group of Tales begins with the Wife of Bath's Prologue and ends with the Franklin's Tale. There is no connection between the Wife's Prologue and the group of stories that precedes; there is no connection between the Franklin's Tale and the group that follows. Within the Marriage Group, on the contrary, there is close connection throughout. That act is a finished act. It begins and ends an elaborate debate. We need not hesitate, therefore, to accept the solution which the Franklin offers as that which Geoffrey Chaucer the man accepted for his own part. Certainly it is a solution that does him infinite credit. A better has never been devised or imagined.

Technology and Deception in *The Canterbury Tales*

Joyce T. Lionarons

References to seemingly magical devices, sub-
stances, powers, and feats appear frequently in
Chaucer's famous collection of pilgrims' tales. In the
following insightful essay, Chaucerian scholar Joyce
T. Lionarons, of Ursinus College, discusses the relationship of magic to technology—and the fact that
both were suspect—in the medieval mind. When it
came to complex new mechanical devices, she
points out, most people perceived only a thin line
between human-made invention and the realm of
magic and the supernatural; therefore, unscrupulous
persons could and did use such inventions to trick
and deceive others, particularly the uneducated.

Chaucer's use of the medieval sciences, and especially of astrological and alchemical lore and terminology, has often
been studied by medievalists seeking to explain the inner
workings of such arts to the modern reader. In particular, a
good deal of attention has been paid to the relationship—perhaps one should say lack of difference—between medieval
science and what may be called pseudo-science, between as-
tronomy and astrology, for example, or chemistry and
alchemy. Rarely, however, do these discussions extend beyond theoretical science to applied science, that is, to the possibly analogous relationship between medieval technology
on the one hand and its pseudo-scientific counterpart, magic,
on the other. That Chaucer was both interested in and knowledgeable about medieval technology is evidenced most
clearly by his [1391] *Treatise on the Astrolabe* [an astrolabe
was a medieval device used to observe and calculate the po-

From Joyce T. Lionarons, "Magic, Machines, and Deception: Technology in the *Can-
terbury Tales*," *Chaucer Review*, vol. 27, no. 4, 1993, pp. 377-85. Copyright 1993 by The
Pennsylvania State University. Reproduced by permission of the Pennsylvania State
University Press.

sition of celestial bodies], but also by the occurrence of technological devices and technical descriptions in both the *Canterbury Tales* and the shorter poetry. He seems to have been less interested in magic, using magical elements where his audience would have expected them—in romances like the *Squire's* or *Franklin's Tale*—but never as the focus of a tale or treatise per se. When one examines Chaucer's poetic usage of both mechanical and magical devices in the *Canterbury Tales* as a whole, however, the line between technology and magic becomes as blurry as that between science and pseudo-science. Technological inventions particularly mechanical devices, frequently function within the *Tales* as if they were in fact magical, while magic often reveals itself to be mechanically based. Magic and technology are alike in that both are based on knowledge hidden from or at least unavailable to the majority of people; this allows each to function within the *Tales* most often as an aid to fraud and trickery.

THE MAGICAL HORSE

Perhaps the most impressive mechanical/magical device in the *Canterbury Tales* is the flying "hors of bras" [brass horse] which a visiting ambassador ... gives to the Mongol king Cambyuskan as one of four apparently magical gifts in the *Squire's Tale*; the other gifts are a mirror that can reveal distant and/or secret events, a ring that gives knowledge of the language of birds and of herbal lore, and a sword that can heal as well as wound. Although we know of no specific source for the tale as a whole, such magical toys are commonplace in medieval romances. ... What is most interesting about Chaucer's version of the flying horse is its distinctly mechanical nature: in order to make it go, the rider must "trille a pyn, stant in his ere" [twirl a peg within his ear]; when it comes time to land, one must "bidde hym descende, and trille another pyn" [bid him descend and twirl another pin]. A third "pyn" causes the horse to "vanysshe anoon / Out of the sighte of every maner wight" [vanish completely from all men's sight]; whether that vanishing is to be interpreted as magical or mechanical is unclear.

Mechanical marvels such as the "hors of bras" have a long history, not only in fictional romances but also in factual accounts of the existence of automata [mechanical devices]. Medieval travelers' tales describe the many types of automata that could be found in the mysterious lands of the

East, creations which were no doubt originally inspired by the technical writings of Philo of Byzantium in the second century B.C. and Hero of Alexandria in the first century A.D., both of which were well known at least to the Arab world of the Middle Ages. Such travelers' accounts include . . . the Throne of Solomon, built by the emperor Theophilus in the ninth century at Constantinople, which featured singing birds made of bronze, a throne which could rise almost to the ceiling, and mechanical lions "who beat the ground with their tails and gave a dreadful roar with open mouth and quivering tongue.". . . For Chaucer's Squire to attribute magical/ mechanical devices to an Arab knight visiting a Mongol court is thus not surprising, whatever background such marvels may have had in romance literature.

Even more interesting than the horse of brass itself, however, is the reaction Chaucer ascribes to the courtiers and common people who come to stare at this marvel in the courtyard: to them it seems "a fairye," a fairy or magical thing, even though it is obviously mechanical, an attitude which seems to suggest that the essence of its magic could be that no one quite understands how it works. No one, we are told, could make the horse move at all, even though the courtiers employ such mundane mechanical devices as windlasses and pulleys: "And cause why?" the Squire asks. "For they ken nat [had not] the craft," he answers.

But even if no one knows precisely how the "magic" horse works, everyone expresses an idea about what kind of magic or technology is entailed here. . . . Some think it is another Pegasus [a flying horse in an ancient Greek myth]; others fear it is a replica of the Trojan horse and has armed warriors inside it. Still others assume it is made by "som magyk, / As jogelours pleyen.". . . We should note that "magyk" is here attributed to jugglers, whose craft is comprised of sleight-of-hand and technical illusion, not to manipulators of supernatural or demonic powers.

To Deceive the Ignorant

Likewise, the other magical toys become objects of technological speculation: perhaps the mirror reveals the unknown . . . the sword must have been tempered in secret ways with a special chemical . . . the knowledge necessary to make the ring was available to Moses and Solomon, but not to ordinary people. The four gifts of the *Squire's Tale* are magical insofar as they all require esoteric knowledge to make or to use, but that knowledge is conceived of as essentially technical; additionally, the mirror and the ring give their users access to hidden or esoteric knowledge. None of the magic in the tale necessarily involves the supernatural; none is clearly differentiated from the technological.

Nevertheless, even if the so-called "magic" is really technology, it is still suspect, precisely *because* it is based on uncommon knowledge and can therefore be used by the learned to deceive the ignorant. This is what the spectators in the *Squire's Tale* are worried about. . . . One can only fully trust that which is commonly known: magic, illusion, and esoteric technology all involve unknown "craft" and are thus potentially dangerous to those lacking the requisite knowledge. Even the language used to define technical inventions can be understood to reflect such dangers: Middle English "gin" can mean either a machine or a deception, "an instance or product of ingenuity, contrivance, scheme, device" or "a cunning stratagem, artifice, trick." Similarly, in the ninth century the Irish monk Martin of Laon derived the Latin *mechanicus* from the Greek *moechus,* adulterer: "From 'moechus' we call 'mechanical art' something clever and most delicate and which, in its making or operation is so invisible that it almost steals the vision of beholders when its ingenuity is not easily penetrated." A mechanical horse could also house armed invaders; the power of a magic mirror could be abused; only by making the "craft" public can the "magic" be diffused and the unlearned be protected. . . .

Sometimes, of course, the potential for deception inherent in illusion and mechanical contrivances could be utilized in a spirit of pure fun. . . . Into this category would fall the elaborate machinery of the Count of Artois's palace at Hesdin, which in the late thirteenth century was equipped with elaborate human and animal automata which could variously speak, beat guests with rods, and/or "spout water and wet people at will." Additionally, there were distorting mirrors, "engiens" to simulate lightning, thunder, rain, and snow, and a gallery featuring "eight pipes for wetting ladies from below and three pipes by which, when people stop in front of them, they are whitened and covered with flour." The equipment for this medieval fun house was apparently kept in repair and in use for close to a full century. . . .

Of course, the use of technology (or magic) to create illusions need not be as innocent as the practical jokes at Hesdin apparently were. The actions of the clerk of Orleans when he agrees to create the illusion that the rocks off the coast of Brittany have been removed in the *Franklin's Tale* are a case in point: his motivation is partly greed, partly pride in his own skill, and partly a desire to help Aurelius fulfill his illicit sexual desires. By creating the illusion that the rocks have disappeared, he not only causes psychological pain to both Dorigen and her husband Arveragus, but he also creates a real physical danger where there was none before by making the potentially perilous rocks invisible to sailors!

It is difficult to pinpoint exactly what the clerk does to create his illusions—the disappearance of the rocks could merely be an unusually high tide—but certain elements within the tale point again to mechanical rather than supernatural magic. . . . Such feats of illusion, created through technical rather than magical means, were often used to entertain dinner guests at medieval feasts. . . .

But of course none of the characters in the *Franklin's Tale* are interested in theatrical entertainments. The men are involved in a joint attempt to deceive Dorigen: the clerk wants money for his labors; Aurelius wants illicit sex. Dorigen herself wants the black rocks to disappear in order to create a comforting illusion that her husband Arveragus is safe. Both Dorigen and Aurelius first turn to prayer to fulfill their desires. . . . But because she realizes she will never gain the knowledge she wants . . . Dorigen concedes that she is powerless and merely prays that God will keep Arveragus safe and, maybe, remove the rocks. Aurelius doesn't give up so easily: he believes he already knows how to get rid of the rocks—by rearranging planetary movements to create a two-year high tide—if only Apollo would cooperate. Failing that, he turns to the secret magical/technical knowledge of the clerk, a man willing to use that knowledge to deceive, but only for a price. For Aurelius or the clerk to act morally within this portion of the tale, both would have to accept, like Dorigen, the limitations of their own knowledge and therefore power in the face of the natural world; instead, they use a technically-produced illusion to create an unnatural and immoral state of affairs.

As in the *Squire's Tale*, the feats performed by the clerk of Orleans go far beyond the limits of true medieval technology, since of course no medieval automata could fly like the

Squire's horse of brass, nor could an illusion on the scale of the clerk's removal of the rocks have been accomplished. Just as in modern science fiction stories, a certain amount of willing suspension of disbelief is necessary to make the technology work. But both tales also illustrate a profound distrust of the technological devices they contain: such devices rely, like magic, on knowledge that is not readily available to common people; like magic, they can be used to deceive the ignorant; perhaps, like magic, they also draw on knowledge improper for human beings to have, since they can tempt a person to try to go beyond the natural limitations of humanity. . . .

THE SECRETS OF ALCHEMY

Moreover, distrust of technology within the *Canterbury Tales* does not seem to be limited to the kind of exotic or arcane machinery necessary to create flying horses or elaborate illusions. Even the most mundane mechanical devices—machines so common and so commonly understood that they have lost all aura of magic—still appear in the tales as aids to deception and fraud. The best example here is Symkyn's mill in the *Reeve's Tale*. The two students arrive to have their corn ground knowing that the miller will try to cheat them; what they don't know is how. They therefore adopt what seems to be the best possible plan under the circumstances: both will watch the mill as closely as possible. . . . Symkyn immediately understands what the clerks are up to, and takes their suspicion as a challenge. He resolves to cheat them as much as he possibly can, in part because he sees the contest as a test of knowledge, his applied, mechanical knowledge against their more abstract, learned "philosophye." Although the clerks, of course, eventually beat the miller at his own game, my point remains constant: mechanical devices in the *Canterbury Tales* are generally at least potential aids to fraud, and those who have knowledge of technology are therefore suspect, no matter how mundane the machinery may be.

It is only in the *Canon Yeoman's Tale*, however, that Chaucer takes this characteristic suspicion of the potential abuses of applied technology to its logical conclusion. The canon/alchemist of the tale proper uses his knowledge of alchemical processes—or perhaps one should say uses the ignorance of others with regard to those processes—in order to deceive; the canon/alchemist of the frame narrative apparently chases after the pilgrims in order to perpetrate some fraud of his own. The Yeoman's revelation of the secrets of both canons follows the pattern we have already seen: those who have technical knowledge, especially if it is secret or in some way exotic, are suspect, as are the devices they construct. Chaucer exhibits such intimate knowledge of both the technical processes of alchemy and the ways in which innocents can be duped that critics have occasionally speculated that he himself was either a master of the art, or an angry dupe determined to avenge himself by revealing all the tricks of the trade. But the tale is far more than a mere warning against alchemy and the potentially duplicitous secrets of alchemical technology, and thus most likely has little to say about Chaucer's own historical involvement with the craft.

TRESPASSING IN GOD'S DOMAIN

It is here that the themes inherent in the four technical/magical gifts of the *Squire's Tale* receive their fullest elucidation, for like those gifts, alchemy both requires esoteric knowledge and promises the initiate access to ever more and greater secrets. It is thus doubly dangerous, as the Yeoman's confessions make clear. If the alchemist could exist like the canon in the tale, using alchemy as a blatantly fraudulent means of acquiring wealth, then merely telling the secrets—educating the unlearned about the technical sleight of hand involved—would suffice to defuse the power of the initiates. But few alchemists can exist that way, or so the Yeoman's self-revelations imply. For alchemy promises much more than technical mastery over a means of deception, more even than a technological way to control the elements of the natural world. It promises to reveal the ultimate secrets of God and nature. . . . And through that promise the alchemist becomes both deceiver and deceived: he deceives others in order to reach his goal; he is himself deceived in the belief that his goal is reachable. . . .

Chaucer's treatment of alchemy thus becomes the clearest example yet of a theme that runs throughout many of the *Canterbury Tales*, that it is dangerous to inquire too closely into secret matters, especially those that may be construed as "Goddes privetee" [God's private domain], that there are types of knowledge that trespass beyond humanity's needs and/or capabilities, and that it is often best merely to accept one's limitations and one's powerlessness and leave control of the natural world to God. . . .

As machines, mechanical devices would seem merely useful; as magic, they can be objects of wonder. But technology is also dangerous. It is dangerous in part because it so often relies on uncommon, new, or secret knowledge and thus can be used to deceive; it is even more dangerous in that it can sometimes deceive the technician into believing that it can provide both god-like control over the natural world and the ultimate answers to philosophical, instead of merely technical, questions. Like the mill in the *Reeve's Tale*, it needs to be watched from both ends.

Romance in *The Canterbury Tales*

J.A. Burrow

Many medieval writers wrote romances, colorful poems and tales about love, chivalry, and adventure; and the most common subject of these works was the legendary world of King Arthur and his knights. Not surprisingly, Chaucer wove the theme of chivalric romance into several of his Canterbury stories. However, as Chaucerian scholar J.A. Burrow, of England's University of Bristol, points out, Chaucer either did not care much for traditional romances or did not want to copy them too closely; as a result, he often used romantic themes in more subtle ways than was usual in his day.

The term 'romance' is not an exact one. Applied to medieval writings it denotes a large area whose outer limits are by no means easy to define. Yet most readers of English literature have some notion of what a typical romance is like, a notion derived mainly from the tales of Arthur and the Round Table. The hero of such a romance will be a knight who engages in perilous adventures, riding out and frequently fighting, sometimes to win or defend a lady, sometimes to defeat enemies of the realm, and sometimes for no evident reason at all. It should be said straightaway that the reader who turns to Chaucer's great story-collection in search of such a typical romance will be disappointed; for the five Canterbury 'romances' to be discussed in this chapter are all, in one way or another, divergent from that stereotype. It is as if Chaucer, who seems so much at home in the fabliau [bawdy comic tale], the miracle of the Virgin, and the saint's life, felt less easy with the very genre which we regard as most characteristic of his period, the knightly romance.

From J.A. Burrow, "The Canterbury Tales I: Romance," in *The Cambridge Chaucer Companion* (New York: Cambridge University Press, 1986). Copyright ©1986 by Cambridge University Press. Reprinted by permission of Cambridge University Press.

THE ARTHURIAN FAIRY WORLD

The only poem of Chaucer which has an Arthurian setting—indeed, the only poem in which he so much as mentions Arthur . . . is the *Wife of Bath's Tale.* The opening line of this tale, 'In th'olde dayes of the Kyng Arthour', holds out the promise that here for once Chaucer is going to try his hand at the most traditional kind of knightly romance. Yet by the end of the poem's first paragraph this expectation is already shaken. . . . The ostensible purpose of [the opening lines] is the same as that of the opening of *Sir Gawain and the Green Knight* [an Arthurian romance by an unknown fourteenth-century poet]: to set the ensuing story in Britain's great age of wonders, the reign of King Arthur. Yet, whereas the *Gawain*-poet's introduction is serious and single-minded, Chaucer's is comic and distracted. It may appear that the Wife of Bath (for the voice is distinctly hers) here turns a traditional comparison upside-down. Arthurian romancers commonly compare modern times unfavourably with the grand old days of Arthur; but the Wife at first speaks as if, for women at least, things are better nowadays. In Arthurian times women lived in continual fear of being raped by the 'elves' or fairy creatures with which the land was then filled; but now these incubi have been driven out by the pious activity of the friars: 'Wommen may go now saufly [safely] up and doun [down]'. This flattery of friars may remind us that the Wife of Bath belongs to that class of 'worthy wommen of the toun' with whom the Friar on the pilgrimage was especially [familiar], according to the *General Prologue.* Such women were, in fact, notorious for their susceptibility to sweet-talking friars. Yet the Wife is a tough character, who can look after herself. Perhaps the Friar's laughing compliment at the end of her prologue irritated her. . . . At any rate, one may detect a note of sarcasm in her response to the Host's call for a tale. . . .

[The Arthurian world in that tale] is essentially a feminine world, dominated by women both human and fairy. The fairy element is not obvious, for the old hag who turns into the beautiful young wife is never explained as an elf-woman. But neither does she turn out to be, as in the three other surviving English versions of the story, a human girl bewitched by a wicked stepmother. Indeed, she is not explained at all. Yet the circumstances in which the knight first encounters her clearly associate her with . . . the queen of the fairies. Under the forest eaves he comes upon a company of four and twenty ladies dancing; and it is after they have mysteriously vanished that he first sees the old hag sitting on the green. This is enough, in a land 'fulfild of fayerye', to establish her true identity.

The dominance of women in the fairy world evoked by the Wife of Bath is striking. The hero of the tale is a man, a 'lusty bacheler' of Arthur's court; but he is not named.... The masculine activities of adventure and feats of arms play no part in his story. Riding back from a day's hawking he commits, it is true, the ultimate act of male domination, when he rapes a passing girl; but, unlike an incubus or a friar, he does not go unpunished. His act of 'oppressioun' delivers him, in fact, into the hands of the women—Arthur's queen and her ladies, and also the elf-woman....

Chaucer's only 'Arthurian romance', then, turns out to be a fairy tale, told by a woman and dominated by women. Perhaps this is how Chaucer thought of Arthurian stories....

A BURLESQUE OF ROMANCE

If this was indeed Chaucer's attitude, it may seem strange that he should have assigned to himself, of all the Canterbury pilgrims, the tale which comes closer than any other of his works to being a story of knightly adventure; but his *Tale of Sir Thopas*, as nearly all readers have noticed, is an outright burlesque. Adventure, as it figured so largely in the romance of chivalry, seems never to have attracted Chaucer's interest.... Having fallen in love with an 'elf-queene', Thopas rides out into the 'contree [country] of Fairye'. There he encounters her monstrous guardian, a three-headed giant called Sir Olifaunt ('Elephant'), whereupon he hurries home again to fetch his armour. There follows an elaborately circumstantial arming scene, very much in the romance manner, after which the knight sets out again to meet the giant. Chaucer is careful to explain that Thopas conducts himself on this second sortie exactly as a ... knight should—sleeping in the open with his helm as a pillow, and drinking nothing but spring water.... At this point, however, the Host can stand no more, and he tells Chaucer to stop.... Perhaps Harry Bailly here voices his creator's thought about those shapeless and interminable adventures which occupy so many medieval romances....

Yet Chaucer's *Sir Thopas* ... [is] a pointed burlesque, not of romance in general, but of the English romances of his day. Modern readers acquainted only with *Sir Gawain and the Green Knight* will miss the immediate point of the joke, for Chaucer's target was a quite different kind of fourteenth-century poem, not much read today but popular in its time: older rhymes such as the romances of Bevis of Hampton and Guy of Warwick (both mentioned in *Sir Thopas*), and newer works such as the two Arthurian pieces composed by Chaucer's contemporary Thomas Chester, *Lybeaus Desconus* and *Sir Launfal.* . . .

MARVELS AND MIRACLES

The next two romances to be considered, those of the Squire and the Franklin, were intended by Chaucer to stand side by side in the completed Canterbury collection. Taken together they may be distinguished from the *Wife of Bath's Tale* and *Sir Thopas* in their treatment of that essential ingredient in romance, the marvellous. Arthurian Britain, according to the Wife of Bath, is a land full of fairy, and the Flanders of Sir Thopas, though comically mundane in itself, abuts upon the 'contree of Fairye'. Both tales accept the fairy as a potent source of marvels which require no further investigation or excuse. Things are different in the Tartary of the *Squire's Tale* and the Brittany of the *Franklin's Tale.* Here wonders have, or may have, natural causes. In the *Squire's Tale* an emissary from the King of Araby and Ind brings four gifts to the Tartar king Cambyuskan and his daughter Canacee, each possessing marvellous powers: a brass horse, an unsheathed sword, a mirror, and a ring. The people of Tartary, so far from accepting these wonders as the commonplaces of romance, look for explanations and precedents. The long passage describing their various speculations shows Chaucer at his best. How can a brass horse fly? Some think it may be 'of Fairye'; others recall the flying horse Pegasus and the wooden horse of Troy. . . . Since the *Squire's Tale* is unfinished, the truth of the matter is never revealed; but we may notice that the most sceptical of the explanations canvassed by the Tartars serves in the *Franklin's Tale* to account for the great marvel of the disappearing rocks. Set the task of removing all the rocks from the coast of Brittany . . . the lovesick squire Aurelius first prays to Apollo for a miracle, but without result; and it is only when he consults a scholar of Orleans who has learned from his books of natural magic the science of producing 'apparences' that Aurelius is able to produce the desired effect. . . .

Although the tales of the Squire and the Franklin are coupled together and share a playful interest in the rationalization of marvels, they are otherwise very different. The *Squire's Tale* presents problems because it is unfinished. . . .

It seems that the *Squire's Tale* was planned as one of those complex, multi-track stories which . . . speak of the 'exquisite intricacies of Arthur'—but with oriental rather than Arthurian materials. Yet the fragmentary condition of the poem leaves its precise character in doubt. The Franklin, by contrast, clearly announces his tale as belonging to that species of romance known as the Breton lay. . . . The Breton lay had its origin in the twelfth century, when minstrels from Brittany performed their 'lays' or songs in the households of France and England. Their lays were essentially musical performances, sung to the harp in the Celtic 'Briton tonge'; but since the emotions they expressed were commonly attributed to characters in stories . . . the performers made a point of explaining the narrative context of their songs in French. . . .

The heart of the *Franklin's Tale* lies elsewhere. Although the Franklin does not share with the Wife and Marie their interest in the fairy, in his tale as in theirs woman plays the dominant role. The chief concern of the tale is with Dorigen and her feelings, and its most characteristic moments are when she piteously laments her absent husband and her present dilemma. In these passages especially the poem comes very close to being another Legend of Good Women. Not for nothing did the Scots poet Gavin Douglas say of his master Chaucer that 'he was evir, God wait, all womanis frend'. Like the Breton lays . . . the *Franklin's Tale* deals above all with [romantic] love: the married love between Dorigen and Arveragus, and the passion of Aurelius for Dorigen. . . .

THE CUSTOMARY HAPPY ENDING

Of all the tales under discussion here the *Knight's Tale* least resembles other medieval romances, French or English. Its source is an Italian poem, the *Teseida* of Giovanni Boccaccio; and the *Teseida* claims to be not a romance but an epic. It is indeed one of the first attempts in a European vernacular to match the twelve-book epics of antiquity. . . . Chaucer, of course, could not incorporate a twelve-book epic in his Canterbury anthology; yet even his version, much abbreviated and with most of the epic machinery removed, is itself a complex and many-sided work, which cannot without discomfort be described simply as a romance.

Literary historians sometimes associate the rise of romance in the twelfth century with the increased interest manifested at that time in individual experience. Certainly the heroes and heroines of [many romances of the period] are activated chiefly by personal considerations, especially the desire for honour and for happiness in love. In this respect, Palamon and Arcite [two knights who are cousins and rivals in the *Knight's Tale*] may be accounted typical romance heroes. Although the *Knight's Tale* is not, like so many of Chaucer's works, dominated by a female character, it is the two young knights' love for Emily which exclusively preoccupies their minds, once they have glimpsed her from their prison window. From that moment on, they are lovers and nothing else, in the best romantic tradition. Their love turns them instantly from sworn brothers into sworn rivals; and it is for love that they fight each other, first in the grove and then at the great tournament. Some readers have seen differences in character between them, but it is doubtful whether Chaucer intended any. . . .

If there were no more to the *Knight's Tale* than this, it might rank as a piece of sentimental courtly casuistry [subtle detail to be ignored]. . . . But the young people in the *Knight's Tale* do not pursue their private ends in isolation: they belong to a larger world with other concerns, best represented by Theseus, Duke of Athens. . . . The Knight begins his tale with Theseus, introducing him as 'lord and governour' of Athens and conqueror of many nations. It is in these capacities that he exerts his influence over the lives of Palamon and Arcite. First, after his conquest of Thebes, he imprisons the two young Theban princes for ever and without hope of ransom—evidently treating them as war criminals along with their dead leader, Creon, who had put himself beyond the pale of humanity by refusing burial to the bodies of the dead. Later, when he comes upon the two young men fighting in the grove, it is Theseus who decrees and organizes the tournament which is to settle their fate. And finally it is Theseus who, after Arcite's death, proposes the marriage between Palamon and Emily, so securing a bond between Athens and Thebes. By these and other actions, Theseus manifests his concern for matters of foreign relations and public order which have no place in romances such as the *Wife of Bath's Tale.* Unlike . . . Arthurian Britain, the Knight's ancient Greece has a political dimension. Its great ceremonial occasions—the tournament . . . the parliament at which Theseus proposes the marriage—are not mere scenes in a romantic pageant. They represent man's attempts to accommodate and civilize the anarchic and inescapable facts of aggression, death, and love, as social life requires. . . .

Theseus speaks not as a philosopher but as a governor, whose business it is to make the best of an awkward human situation, and who is also . . . interested in linking the royal houses of Athens and Thebes by marriage. He is so little a philosopher that, in flat contradiction of his earlier argument, he can go on to offer Emily and Palamon the prospect of 'o parfit joye, lastynge everemo' [one perfect joy, lasting forever] in their marriage.

The *Knight's Tale* does indeed end in the 'parfit joye' of mutual love in marriage. . . .

PALAMON AND EMILY ARE MARRIED

This excerpt is taken from J.U. Nicolson's translation of The Canterbury Tales.

Between them, then, was tied that nuptial band,
Which is called matrimony or marriage,
By all the council and the baronage.
And thus, in all bliss and with melody,
Has Palamon now wedded Emily.
And God, Who all this universe has wrought,
Send him His love, who has it dearly bought.
For now has Palamon, in all things, wealth,
Living in bliss, in riches, and in health;
And Emily loved him so tenderly,
And he served her so well and faithfully,
That never word once marred their happiness,
No jealousy, nor other such distress.
Thus ends now Palamon and Emily;
And may God save all this fair company! Amen.

This is the customary happy ending of romance. Each of the two other Canterbury romances completed by Chaucer leaves its hero and heroine united in the same fairy-tale felicity: 'parfit joye' in the *Wife of Bath's Tale*, 'sovereyn blisse' in the *Franklin's Tale*. Yet it is a measure of the greater seriousness of the *Knight's Tale* that the happy ending here seems a fragile and questionable thing, shadowed by thoughts of suffering and death and especially by the memory of Arcite's [modernized] dying words:

> What is this world? What asks a man to have? Now with his love, now in the cold dark grave alone, with never any company.

CHAPTER 3

Specific Characters and Stories in *The Canterbury Tales*

READINGS ON
THE CANTERBURY TALES

Sketches of the Characters in *The Canterbury Tales*

Marchette Chute

In this excerpt from her book *Geoffery Chaucer of England*, Marchette Chute, a noted scholar of medieval and Elizabethan literature, presents an overview of the main characters of *The Canterbury Tales*. After commenting on the setting of the pilgrimage in which Chaucer places these characters, Chute provides thumbnail sketches of the stalwart Knight, the gentle Prioress, the gregarious Friar, the learned Clerk, and many of the other members of the pilgrim company, finally reaching the repulsive Summoner and unscrupulous Pardoner, who bring up the rear of the group. Chute's concise and colorful descriptions of Chaucer's gallery of medieval men and women serves both as a starting point and a ready reference for the more detailed explorations of individual characters that follow.

No one knows when Chaucer began to write *The Canterbury Tales*, much less when the idea of writing it first came to him. Perhaps he thought of it suddenly one day when he was among the crowd of travelers that used the busy road between London and Canterbury. Perhaps ... the idea of writing a collection of stories told by pilgrims had been in his mind for several years before he put it down on paper.... Whenever the idea for *The Canterbury Tales* came to Chaucer, it came obviously as a product of his full maturity as an artist....

There is a lifetime of observation packed into *The Canterbury Tales*, and never was a work of art more unmistakably the product of the whole man.

From *Geoffrey Chaucer of England* by Marchette Chute. Copyright ©1946 by E.P. Dutton. Copyright ©1974 by Marchette Chute. Used by permission of Dutton Signet, a division of Penguin Books USA Inc.

CHARACTERS DRAWN FROM LIFE

The peculiar merit of the structure of *The Canterbury Tales* was that it gave Chaucer an opportunity to use everything he possessed. Once the original idea was conceived of an assorted group of people going on a journey together and each one expected to tell a story, the possibilities were endless. Everything Chaucer knew about people could be included in it, for the design was elastic enough to include a thick-necked miller and a refined prioress and a middle-class doctor and a rowdy cook and an embroidered squire and a fat cloth-maker. Everything that Chaucer knew about poetry could go into it also, for every mood could be represented from romance to farce. . . .

Chaucer never finished the poem; his magnificent plan was still much more in his head than it was on paper when he had to leave it. . . . Some of the characterizations are complete but some are hardly more than sketched in, and the tales are not in order. *The Canterbury Tales* as it stands now is only a collection of fragments. The fragments have been tentatively arranged in some sort of order by later editors, all of whom naturally disagree with each other, but nothing definitive can be done with the series of unfinished sketches that survived into the fifteenth century as Chaucer's legacy. Yet for all that, Chaucer completed enough of *The Canterbury Tales* to make it one of the literary masterpieces of the world, and he visualized his characters so clearly that after the dust of six centuries they are still as real and as familiar as the day they met each other at the Tabard Inn.

So real, in fact, are the twenty-nine pilgrims who rode with Chaucer to Canterbury that it has been suggested that the poet was describing actual contemporaries of his. . . . Some of his pilgrims Chaucer certainly drew from life in the sense that some real human being started the picture forming in his mind that eventually emerged as an independent artistic creation. No artist works in a vacuum, and no doubt somewhere in Elizabethan England walked the man who first made Shakespeare think of Falstaff. But this is not to say that Chaucer was consciously picking out real people from among his acquaintances, with real names and addresses, and that he expected his readers to identify them as such. He knew that the Miller had a wart on his nose and that the Monk's sleeves were trimmed with fur at the wrist and that the Reeve had a grey horse named Scot and that the Shipman's boat was called the *Magdalen*. . . .

At any rate, whether Chaucer's pilgrims actually once walked the streets in the towns to which he assigned them or whether it was the poet himself who gave them a local habitation and a name, the important fact remains that they are alive now. They have walked out of England and into immortality because they were born of a universal rather than a contemporary truth, and they are citizens now of a more enduring town than either London or Bath. . . .

The characters whom Chaucer had time to develop fully, like the Pardoner and the Prioress and the Wife of Bath, take on a depth of reality that no other writer in England but Shakespeare ever surpassed. Chaucer is of course no Shakespeare, but in this respect he came nearer him than any other poet, and even the best of later novelists and dramatists are usually not a match for him here.

It can be put down to inspiration that Chaucer hit upon an idea for a major poem that would make use of his profound knowledge of character, but the fact that he could make full use of the idea after it came to him must be attributed to a lifetime of disciplined respect for the art of poetry. . . .

THE TRAVELERS MEET AT THE TABARD INN

The poem opens in April. It is the season when the birds start to sing and the world turns green, and everyone suddenly wants to go traveling. The tourist impulse was frowned upon in the Middle Ages if one took to the road merely for one's own amusement, but it was very respectable if one ended with a visit to the shrine of a saint. Theoretically this was done in a spirit of humble devotion; the pilgrim journeyed on foot, clad in a grey cloak, with a scrip and a pilgrim staff to proclaim his intentions. In actual practice, however, a pilgrimage worked out quite differently, and in the fourteenth century a trip of this kind was much more likely to be one of cheerful sightseeing than of devout meditation.

England was full of shrines, from one end of the realm to the other, but the most popular of all these holy attractions was the shrine of the murdered Archbishop of Canterbury, Thomas à Becket. Relics of the twelfth-century saint were scattered everywhere . . . but it was in the great cathedral at Canterbury that he had worked and died, and the blood of his martyrdom was still visible before the altar. There were monks to guide each new band of pilgrims, to show them the banners and the painted glass and the holy shrine in Trinity Chapel which probably had more jeweled wealth loaded into a single spot than anywhere else in England. The street that led to the cathedral was called Mercery Lane, and it was lined with shops where the pilgrims could buy souvenirs to take home with them.

The road through London was the natural thoroughfare for pilgrims from the north of England. They could pause to visit St. Paul's churchyard, where Thomas à Becket's father and mother were buried, and pray for a moment in the beautiful little two-story chapel on London Bridge that was also dedicated to London's most famous citizen. Then the average pilgrim would spend the night at Southwark, just on the other side of the bridge, so that he could avoid the early morning traffic into the city when he set out for Canterbury.

On this particular evening in April, twenty-nine people were lodged at the Tabard Inn in Southwark on their way to Canterbury the next morning, and Chaucer says that he spoke with them all.

While this is unquestionably what Geoffrey Chaucer himself would have done, it is not the real Chaucer who makes his appearance in *The Canterbury Tales*. It is "Geoffrey," the same fat, well-meaning, not very intelligent individual who was so thoroughly lectured by the Eagle in [Chaucer's earlier work] *The House of Fame*. Geoffrey has become, if anything, slightly more feeble-minded with the passage of the years, for he is the only one among the pilgrims who is incapable of offering a presentable tale in rhyme. He does his best, but his best is so dreadful that the Host is obliged to stop him in the middle of it because the pilgrims can stand no more; and therefore Geoffrey, who is certainly Chaucer's favorite butt, is reduced to telling "a litel thyng in prose."

THE UNMEDIEVAL PROLOGUE

Chaucer does not draw Geoffrey's portrait in the Prologue; but he makes up for this omission by the vividness and accuracy with which he supplies the portraits of everyone else.

To realize the exact extent of Chaucer's achievement in the Prologue to *The Canterbury Tales*, it is necessary to remember that the Middle Ages was not a time of portraits. It was a time of patterns, of allegories, of reducing the specific to the general and then drawing a moral from it. An occasional poet had shown his ability to draw a picture in sharp, factual and occasionally comic detail . . . and some of the London preachers were in the habit of enlivening their sermons with anecdotes that they brightened with local color and a few highly realistic touches. . . .

What Chaucer was doing was entirely different. As a major creative artist he had set himself to draw, with serious, factual . . . exactness, the portraits of twenty-nine people. He did not set out to be moral. He did not even set out to be entertaining. He merely set out to be accurate, so that each of the twenty-nine would be as vivid to the reader as he was to Chaucer himself. . . .

Chaucer threw the whole book of rules overboard in his Prologue. He even refused to obey the regulation, almost sacred by this time, which prescribed that a description should begin in an orderly manner and work from one end of the man or woman described to the other. When Chaucer describes his Miller, for instance, he leaps, with the appearance of doing it almost at random, from his prowess as a wrestler, to his red beard, to the tuft of bristles on his nose, to his sword, to the size of his mouth, to his business methods, to his hood, to his bagpipes. This is not done at random, of course. It is done deliberately, to give an effect of such reality that a man and not a pattern stands in front of the reader. Chaucer's method was unmedieval and so was his purpose. The two combine to make the Prologue to *The Canterbury Tales* unlike anything that had ever been written before in Christendom.

THE KNIGHT AND HIS FOLLOWERS

Chaucer begins with a Knight. Chaucer's Knight was everything that a knight should be and usually was not—honorable, courteous to all classes, gallant in war and very conscientious about the religious significance of a pilgrimage. He may have been . . . a composite portrait of some of Chaucer's own friends. Nevertheless the Knight is not a type but a real individual. Chaucer knows exactly how many battles he fought and where, what kind of horse he rode, and even the way the metal on his coat of mail has marked his tunic underneath.

The Knight's son, the Squire, was also everything that he should be. A proper courtly lover, he had fought for his lady's smile in Flanders and Picardy, and he knew how to sing and dance and joust and write love lyrics as any well-educated young gentleman should. He was dressed in the latest fashion, his locks were so neatly curled they might have been laid in a press, and he reminded Chaucer of a field full of daisies.

These two aristocrats had an efficient servant along with them. He was clad in green, with his dagger well-sharpened and his arrows tipped with peacock feathers. He does not open his mouth in any of the subsequent conversations, but Chaucer is of the opinion he was a forester because there is a silver image of St. Christopher, the patron saint of foresters, hanging upon his breast.

THE PRIORESS, THE MONK, AND THE FRIAR

Next comes Chaucer's famous Prioress. Hers is so delicate, subtle and affectionate a portrait that it deserves special mention.... It is a superlative example of how the very soul of a woman may be built up through a series of skillfully chosen objective details. Flaubert, however, could not have smiled in print if his life depended upon it, while Chaucer cannot prevent himself from teasing the Prioress a little even while he loves her.

Madame Eglantine was a perfect lady, and well she knew it in her gently complacent way. She spoke French very well, although not, it is true, with a Parisian accent. Her wimple was just so, her nose was elegantly formed, and her table manners were charming. She kept several little dogs, whom she spoiled by giving them the kind of food that puppies are not supposed to eat, and she had so tender a heart that she wept if she looked at a dead mouse caught in a trap....

Chaucer's portrait of the Monk is very much less gentle and somewhat less subtle, but there is the same skill in the handling of objective detail in order to arouse a specific emotional response in the reader. The Monk was one of those full-feeding sportsmen that occur in every age, and he had no intention of letting the fact that he was in holy orders interfere with his fondness for hunting or for roast goose. Chaucer agrees with bland politeness that of course St. Augustine was wrong; quite the best thing any monk can do is to keep a pack of greyhounds and a stable full of horses, and to ride about the country with his bridle bells jingling, his bald head shining, and a gold love knot under his fat chin.

Equally courteous are Chaucer's remarks about the Friar. For the Friar was a fine figure of a man, with his thick white neck and his easy manners, and it was quite natural that he should have more acquaintances among the tavern keepers of a town than among the sick and the poor. For what kind of "avaunce" [profit] could a man get by making the acquaintance of a leper? His tippet was stuck full of knives and pins, which he used to establish intimate relations with the young ladies of the town, and he lisped a little because he thought it sounded fetching. He had a remarkable talent for extracting money from the unwilling, his eyes twinkled like the stars on a frosty night, and his name was Huberd.

A GALLERY OF PROFESSIONAL MEN

Next came the Merchant, a member of a class that Chaucer had reason to know intimately. He had a forked beard and a high saddle, a beaver hat and a pair of excellently fitting boots. His soul was chiefly occupied with pride over his business successes and worry over the lack of security of Channel shipping, and Chaucer was not really very fond of him.

Chaucer was very fond, however, of the Clerk. The Clerk spent all his money on books and Chaucer's heart went out to him. With his shabby coat and thin horse he was the kind of man who never gets on in the world and enrages more successful people by not minding. The Clerk's own idea of success was to have twenty books at the head of his bed where he could reach them easily. Chaucer said of him,

Gladly would he lerne [learn] and gladly teche [teach],

which is the handsomest compliment that one lover of books could give to another.

Next came a Man of Law, a class that Chaucer knew as well as he knew merchants. This particular individual was a sergeant at law, and had identified himself so thoroughly with his profession that he had lost some of his interest as a human being. He was a distinguished lawyer but there was nothing inside. However, he was adept in real estate deals and could quote every legal decision that had been handed down since William the Conqueror.

A much more affectionate portrait is that of the Franklin. The Franklin was a freeholder, a member of the county gentry of the kind that Chaucer encountered so frequently in Kent. A solid sort of Englishman, he had presided many times over local meetings of the justices of the peace and had represented his county frequently in Parliament as a knight of the shire. The Franklin was not a profound man, but he was good company and very fond of guests. He was also very fond of eating—in fact, he was an expert on the subject of food—and his beard was as white as a daisy flower.

There were five guild members from various London professions, new enough to wealth so that their outfits had been freshly bought. They were all rich enough to be aldermen and their wives were all hoping they would be elected; for, as Chaucer says, it is delightful to be called "madame" and to be given precedence at the guild festivities.

The five guildsmen brought along a Cook with them. He was not a private cook but the proprietor of a cook-shop, which was a combination restaurant and delicatessen. The Cook was skilled in his profession, in spite of the insults he had to endure on the subject from his fellow pilgrims, and he knew all there was to know about the mashed and heavily spiced foods that were popular in a period of no forks and little refrigeration. He was a little too fond of London ale, and it was perhaps on that account that he had a bad ulcer on his shin.

There was also a Shipman, riding uncomfortably upon that alien method of travel, a horse. The Merchant must have eyed him a little thoughtfully, for the Shipman was not above stealing part of the wine cargoes that he was supposed to ship across the Channel. He lived somewhere near Dartmouth, which Chaucer knew by personal experience was notable for its pirates, and after a naval battle he left the defeated side to walk home by water. Apart from his elastic morals he was a good mariner, for he knew even the little-known waterways of Spain. He had a fine coat of tan and wore his dagger on a string around his neck.

Another very successful professional was the Doctor. The practice of medicine was a lucrative one in fourteenth-century England, and the plague had made Chaucer's Doctor a rich man. He deserved to be, for he was a very learned one. . . . The Doctor was very fond of gold, but this, says Chaucer, was of course because gold has such excellent medicinal properties.

THE WIFE OF BATH, FOLLOWED BY TWO BROTHERS

The next pilgrim was the Wife of Bath. . . . It is not until the lady swings into action that her remarkable qualities become evident, but even the brief portrait in the Prologue makes it clear that here is no ordinary woman.

Everyone knows her red face and her broad hat, her scarlet stockings and the outer riding skirt that she wears wrapped around her broad hips. She was already an old hand at pilgrimages, for she liked "felaweships" [fellowships] and gadding about and had taken three times the long trip to Jerusalem. The Wife of Bath had gone through five husbands, not counting "oother compaignye" [other company, that is, boyfriends] in her youth, and she had a high opinion of her gifts as a weaver and her social standing in the suburb of Bath where she lived. It was an unwise woman who tried to precede her when the offerings were made in church on Sunday. She was a little deaf (a fact that may have had something to do with her unparalleled gifts as a monologist) and there were gaps between her teeth.

After her came a Plowman and his brother, a Parson. They were both very good men, and it is sad that they should be so much less interesting. The Plowman was everything he ought to be; he loved his neighbors and paid his taxes and worked hard, and some of Chaucer's fellow landowners in Kent probably read the description with the same sort of disbelief that a modern capitalist might give to a similar portrait of a modern workman.

The Parson is a more interesting man than his brother, for Chaucer describes him in greater detail. He was well educated, as a peasant could be in the Middle Ages if he wanted to, but his learning had not made him restless. He labored through the thunder and the rain from one end of his large parish to the other, and never thought of the easy money that could be made by going up to London and establishing himself in a chantry to pray for some dead merchant's soul. He preferred to give money to his parishioners instead of taking it away from them and refused even to "cursen for his tithes" [threaten to excommunicate people if they did not pay the tithe, or church tax]. He was in sharp contrast to the Friar, whose courtesy towards the rich was a wonder to behold, in that he would "snybben" [sharply criticize] a wealthy man without hesitation if he thought he deserved a reproof. The Parson was a most uncommon ecclesiastic, gentle to the poor and austere only with the rich. . . .

SEVERAL LOW-CLASS FELLOWS

The rest of the company consisted of five extremely low-class individuals, with Chaucer himself bringing up the rear.

The first of these is the Miller, upon whom Chaucer lavishes a minutely realistic description worthy of a Flemish portrait painter of the following century. The Miller was a heavy-set fellow, with thick shoulders and a head so hard he could break a door with it. He had a red, spade-shaped beard, and the tuft of hairs that stood up from a wart on his nose were as red as the bristles in a sow's ear. He had wide black nostrils, and was both an accomplished stealer of corn and a teller of dirty stories. He wore a white coat and a blue hood, and led the pilgrims out of town by blowing on his bagpipes.

The next of the five was the Manciple ... a purchasing agent, responsible for buying the provisions for the lawyers; and while they were a "heep of lerned men," Chaucer's Manciple was clever enough to make fools of them all.

Another agent was the Reeve. His function was that of general manager for a country estate, a business he managed so efficiently that no auditor could frighten him and he earned his lord's thanks by lending back to him his own money. He had trained in his youth to be a carpenter, and came from Norfolk just outside the town of Baldeswell. He wore his beard cropped as close as he could get it, with his head shorn like a priest's, and his legs were so thin that they showed no calf at all. He wore his long coat hitched up and held by a girdle and he kept always to the rear end of the procession.

The Reeve was a crook, but he was a man of high virtue in comparison to the Summoner and the Pardoner, the two individuals who complete the list....

The Summoner was a member of the group that made a living out of citing delinquents to appear before the papal court. He was ... the kind who would lend out his girl for a twelvemonth in exchange for a quart of wine. His face was blotched with a skin disease, so that children were terrified of him, and he had scabby eyebrows and slits of eyes. His breath was always heavy with garlic and onions and he yelled like a madman when he was drunk. His head was decorated with a garland for the occasion and he carried a large cake as a shield. He also supplied the refrain in a trumpeting voice while his dear friend the Pardoner sang, "Come hither, love, to me."

The Pardoner had been sent out by a hospital near Charing Cross to raise money by selling papal indulgences. He had flat yellow hair, as yellow as wax, which hung down in limp strips over his shoulders, and he wore no hood upon it because he believed this to be the latest fashion. He had star-

ing eyes and a voice as thin as a goat's and because he was
sexually abnormal he had not been able to grow a beard. He
was well supplied with the tools of his trade, for he had a
glass full of "pigges bones," a piece of Saint Peter's sail, and
a pillowcase which he said had belonged to Our Lady. With
these appliances he could go into a church and raise more
money in a day than the local parson collected in a month.

SURPASSING THE STANDARDS OF HIS AGE

In introducing men of this kind into serious poetry, Chaucer
was running directly counter to the whole spirit of his age.
He had no moral purpose in describing the Pardoner, and no
religious purpose. He described the Pardoner merely because the man was like that, which was a Renaissance point
of view and not a medieval one. . . .

Nor did Chaucer present his erring pilgrims as a moralist
might, illustrating various aspects of sin so that his audience
might draw the necessary moral. He suggested no moral.
There was none to suggest. He merely described people as
they were. [For this, he apologized, claiming, "My wit is
short, you may well understand."] . . .

There is no doubt that Chaucer found a most convenient
literary refuge in his pet legend that he was short of wit. He
could use it whenever he wanted to do something that he
was not supposed to do. According to this convenient fiction
he was merely a fat, well-intentioned man, not at all bright,
who happened to be going on a pilgrimage in April, met a
mixed group of people at an inn, and carefully set down on
paper what each of them looked like and what they said. The
Canterbury pilgrims were not his; he merely met them at an
inn. *The Canterbury Tales* were not his; he merely overheard
them.

There was probably no one in Chaucer's audience who
actually believed this fiction, but it had the virtue of disarm-
ing criticism. No one can be severe with an author who
starts out by cheerfully proclaiming himself to be a fool.

The device of disclaiming responsibility for both the pilgrims and the tales leaves Chaucer free to do what he likes
with them. The Pardoner and the Reeve, the Miller and the
Wife of Bath, are able to behave as a great realist wished
them to . . . in accordance with Chaucer's own standards
rather than with the standards of his age.

The *Knight's Tale:* A Stately Story of Uneven Justice

Michael Stevens

The *Knight's Tale* is arguably one of the three or four most famous of all the stories in Chaucer's Canterbury collection. On the surface, the tale appears to be a straightforward presentation of the kind of colorful jousting and romance depicted in earlier European legends of chivalry such as those of King Arthur and his knights. However, according to Chaucerian scholar Michael Stevens, coauthor of *Chaucer's Major Tales,* under the surface the *Knight's Tale* is a philosophical exploration of the concept of unequal justice. Chaucer's main point, says Stevens, is that to Providence, or the hand of God, goodness and justice are the same; while to human beings, by contrast, these two virtues can often be mutually exclusive. Thus, while the death of one of the two seemingly equally worthy knights may seem somehow unjust, it is also good in the sense that it leads to lifelong happiness for the other knight and his bride.

At the Host's request the pilgrims draw lots to decide who should tell the first tale, and it is no great coincidence that 'the cut fil to the Knyght' [the lot fell to the Knight] whom Chaucer portrays as representing the highest ideals of medieval Christian chivalry. He combines in his person and his office all the virtue of a devout Christian, of a respected member of the nobility and of a military commander skilled in the use of arms and experienced in foreign travel. As one would expect in the Age of Chivalry there is great emphasis laid upon the glory of war, but it must be remembered that the wars he fought in were the Holy Crusades [which took place several centuries after the chivalrous age of the King

From *Chaucer's Major Tales* by Michael Hoy and Michael Stevens. Copyright ©1969 by Michael Hoy and Michael Stevens. Reprinted by permission of Schocken Books, published by Pantheon Books, a division of Random House, Inc.

Arthur legends]. . . . He is, therefore, a particularly appropriate character to start the series off and to set a pattern for all the stories that follow.

The elevated rhetorical style so appropriate to this 'noble storie' and to its dignified narrator is adopted at the outset and maintained throughout, and is a great contrast to the colloquial informality of 'The General Prologue' and many of the other tales. This Tale opens with the conventional rhetorical reference to authority ('as olde stories tellen [tell] us') and we are straightaway introduced to the epic character of Duke Theseus who, like the Knight himself, is returning victorious from the wars when he is waylaid by the Theban wives. But even in the compassion shown by Theseus for their predicament, very little warmth of character is displayed. It is all very formal, with the introduction of a . . . revenge theme and with the wailing women themselves behaving more like the Chorus in a classical [ancient Greek] drama than as fellow human beings who engage our sympathy. . . . With all the formality and ritual of tragic drama we are introduced right at the beginning to the central theme of 'The Knight's Tale' with the noble duke 'In al his wele and in his mooste pride' [In all his glory and greatest pride] suddenly being made aware of the sufferings of others. . . .

Inevitably the uncomplicated plot of 'The Knight's Tale' prompts the philosophical question of why Providence, who is all good, should allow one of two cousins of identical circumstances of birth and fortune to die, while the other is allowed to remain [living]. . . . It is the same question which the sixth-century Roman thinker Anicius Manlius Boethius had considered in his *De Consolatione Philosophiae*, which takes the form of a dialogue between Boethius and his 'nurse' Philosophy. After proving to him that both blessedness and God are the chiefest good, Philosophy goes on to say:

> Providence is the very Divine reason itself, seated in the highest Prince, which disposeth of all things. But Fate is a disposition inherent in changeable things, by which Providence connecteth all things in their due order. 'Perceivest thou now what followeth?' [she asked]. 'What?' [said I]. 'That' [quoth she], 'all manner of fortune is good'.

And after proving that nothing happens by chance, Philosophy goes on:

> Ought, then, by parity of reason, all things to be just because He is just who willed them to be? That is not so either. For to be good involves Being, to be just involves an act. For him

being and action are identical; to be good and to be just are
one and the same for Him. But being and action are not identical for us, for we are not simple. For us, then, goodness is
not the same thing as justice, but we all have the same sort of
Being in virtue of our existence. Therefore all things are
good, but all things are not just. Finally, good is general, but
just is a species, and this species does not apply to all. Where-
fore some things are just, others are something else, but all
things are good.

These stoical views influenced Chaucer considerably and he
incorporates them in several of his works, but none with
more irony than in 'The Knight's Tale'.... The emphasis is on
man's behaviour 'in this world' and there is no suggestion either in Boethius or in Chaucer of the possibility of redemption
in a life after death ... [no] hint of any Christian doctrine....

Chaucer's Knight, having his own precise place in the feudal hierarchy, with its concern for order in society, would, despite Theseus's lack of any overt Christianity, have had some
fellow-feeling for the Duke, who is the character through
whom all the philosophic pronouncements are made. 'Providence is the very Divine reason itself, seated in the highest
Prince, which disposeth of all things', says Boethius, and this
is the Duke's own function in the Tale, disposing on earth by
a kind of Divine Right, the authority of [God]....

THE INEQUALITY OF JUSTICE

After the variety of the portraits in 'The General Prologue' it
is, perhaps, surprising that the characters in the first Tale
should be presented in such a formalized manner. Theseus
himself is the only one to stand out as an individual and, as
we have already seen, he is introduced at the outset as little
more than an actor in a stylised ritualistic drama, and the
mouthpiece for the philosophical content of the poem. Nevertheless, as the Tale develops he emerges as a character
who asserts his authority, but does so with restraint and humanity. It would, indeed, have been inappropriate to differ-
entiate too obviously between Palamon and Arcite, for to
have done so would have been to weaken the examination of
the apparent inequality of the justice meted out by Providence, which is the theme of the Tale. As personalities, of
course, there is some difference. The love which Palamon,
who symbolises the whole conception of romantic Courtly
Love, bears for Emily is on a more exalted plane than that of
his rival, who symbolises the chivalric military code ... and

we are satisfied that each has an equal right to the lady's affections even if Palamon did see her first. . . . When viewed objectively there is little to choose between the claims of the two lovers, but it is the difference in their temperaments that will determine our support for one rather than the other. Palamon appears to have the purer motives, is more of a visionary who worships Emily as a goddess, and goes to pray for her in the temple of Venus [goddess of love]. Arcite is more the worldly man of action, showing much greater initiative during his freedom by organizing his return in disguise to Theseus's court to be near Emily, and he is the warrior who prays to Mars [god of war] for victory.

The characters of these two young men are presented in the same kind of two-dimensional form as the characters in a [Franz] Kafka novel where there is the same preoccupation with a sense of justice as imposed by a bureaucratic government. Kafka's novels have been interpreted as prophetic political allegories foretelling the plight of central European Jewry in the mid-twentieth century. It is tempting to view 'The Knight's Tale' in a similar way as anticipating by some seven or eight years the tragic events which marked the close of Richard II's reign, with the contrasted personalities of the cousins Palamon and Arcite representing the conflict between the visionary, self-indulgent king and his politically ambitious, military-minded cousin, Henry Bolingbroke. The closing events of this reign, too, were determined by the settlement of the argument between two disputant knights in a trial by arms arranged by the highest authority in the land, which then banished them as Arcite was banished by Duke Theseus. Further point is given to the satire when one realizes that the red and white of Theseus's banner are also King Richard's own livery colours. There could also be some double-edged irony in the fact that, although Arcite is victorious in the feat of arms, it brings him little lasting earthly reward.

AUTHENTIC AND REALISTIC DESCRIPTIONS

To say that 'The Knight's Tale' is deficient in the subtle delineation of the characters as complex individuals, is not to deny the Tale considerable narrative force. Chaucer tells us that it was universally popular among the pilgrims themselves, appealing especially to the 'gentils' in the company. For the modern reader some 'willing suspension of disbelief' is necessary, but we need not, as has been suggested, give ourselves over entirely to the world of faery and romance to offset the apparent lack of characterization and probability of action. A triangular love contest is as popular as ever it was, and the lack of characterization does not diminish the interest. We are just as curious to know who is going to win in the end, and the delaying of the action by the colourful build-up to the big fight creates considerable suspense.

If the theme of the Tale is to wrestle with an abstract problem of philosophy, the philosopher and the poet realize that the problem has to be resolved 'in this world' so the story itself is set against the most concrete of backgrounds described in some of the most forceful poetry in the language. The authentic world of medieval tourney is described with the arrival of Lycurgus and Emetrius, the two knights in attendance on Palamon and Arcite respectively. These are two more symbolic figures representing the pomp and power of majesty, but Chaucer does not deny them their own peculiar physical characteristics. Of Lycurgus he says [in modernized translation]:

> Black was his beard, and manly was his face.
> The circles of his eyes in his head
> Burned in a glow between yellow and red:
> And like a griffin he looked about,
> With shaggy hairs on his heavy brows;
> His limbs massive, his muscles hard and strong,
> His shoulders broad, his arms heavy and long.

And of Emetrius:

> His curly hair ran into rings,
> And that was yellow, and glittered like the sun.
> His nose was prominent, his eyes bright green-yellow,
> His lips full, his color was ruddy,
> A few freckles spotted his face,
> Colored somewhere between yellow and black,
> And like a lion he cast his looks.

The world of romance may be emphasized by the comparison with the heraldic gryphon and lion, but the other physical details such as the coarse facial hairs and glowing eyes of the one and the freckles of the other are as acute and realistic as anything in 'The General Prologue', while the reference to the colours would have especial significance to a medieval audience. Nor does the symbolical function of the other characters cause Chaucer to disregard entirely physical differences: Palamon is distinguished by his 'flotery berd and ruggy, asshy heeres', Arcite is 'long and big of bones' and Emily has her yard-long golden tresses crowned with a garland of flowers. Realism abounds in the graphic detailed descriptions of the pre-tournament preparations.... This is as authentic and realistic as Shakespeare's account in *Henry V* of the preparations in the English camp before the battle of Agincourt.... Here the bold alliterative verse with its Anglo-Saxon vocabulary and the emphatically strong verbs and end-stopped lines conveys all the ferocity of the conflict which is perfectly suited to the epic and heroic atmosphere of the Tale.

The sudden and unexpected reversal of fortune at the height of Arcite's success is dismissed rapidly, but the tension mounts with the minutiae of the medical details of his fatal injury. The same extravagance is expended on Arcite's funeral preparations as were lavished during his life, and his corpse is bedecked with cloth of gold.

These lengthy descriptions themselves, together with the long speeches of Theseus, have been considered by some as contributing to the apparent lack of verisimilitude [realism] in the Tale. It should, however, be clear from the language that the poet is realistically depicting the virile, masculine medieval world in which he lived; but, in order to accord with his ironic treatment of Boethian ideas, emphasizing the stress his contemporaries laid upon worldly externals and neglecting to some extent the importance they also attached to spiritual values. The pronouncements of Theseus do tend to slow up the tempo of the poem at times, seldom carrying the action any further forward, but a slow majestic pace is not inappropriate to the dignified theme of the Tale and is in keeping, not only with the character of Theseus, but also with the Knight himself whom we can imagine as being slow and ponderous at times, yet terse at others, and particularly exuberant when recounting any military exploits. In any case, although the elevated tone is maintained throughout the Tale, it is relieved by some colloquial touches and homely dialogue....

CIRCUMSTANCES BEYOND OUR CONTROL

A striking feature of this Tale is the degree of unity and balance in its structure. The arrangement of all the characters in the Tale is perfectly balanced. The two earthly knights of identical status, who strive for the love of the same lady, are paralleled in the supernatural world by Venus (Palamon),

Mars (Arcite) and Diana (Emily), and are presided over by Saturn, who performs the same judicial role on this plane as Theseus on earth.... This sense of order and stability is conveyed throughout by Duke Theseus. He redresses the balance by avenging the deaths of the Theban husbands, he resolves the quarrel between the two lovers by elevating the scene from a backwoods brawl to one with all the magnificent pomp and splendour of a royal tournament within the rigid rules of courtly conduct, and he unites Palamon and Emily in Christian marriage with all due decorum. The lists, which he orders to be built, are circular in shape and there is complete uniformity in the arrangement of the altars and the temples, each of which is described in the same logical way; Lycurgus and his retinue of exactly one hundred knights balances that of Emetrius and his equal number of followers, and the whole procedure adopted by the contestants before the tournament is identical. In the funeral procession old Egeus balances Theseus. The precise numerical details all help to stress the concern for regularity.... This enormous emphasis on the structural unity of the Tale helps to cloak some of the ambivalence in the philosophical doctrine behind the story itself with its overriding belief that man is subject to all the irrational whimsicalities of Dame Fortune....

Of all the *Canterbury Tales* this opening story which superficially appears to be a straightforward conventional medieval romance within the framework of contemporary thought, is one of the most difficult to evaluate. It is, with certain reservations, an appealing short story, but with all its spectacular settings it is clearly no mere glittering pageant of courtly life in the Middle Ages. Like a great Gothic cathedral with its pinnacled spires reaching skywards into the unknown, it reflects the medieval preoccupation with the great questions of human existence.... Writing in an age so concerned with degree and the order of Nature, Chaucer has infused Boccaccio's story with the concepts of Boethian philosophy in order to discuss the universal problem of man's endurance in the face of circumstances that are beyond his control. Human beings caught up in the great political issues of the twentieth century are presented with the same heart-searching doubts and ... this is the Stoic wisdom that 'The Knight's Tale' teaches [us].

Chaucer's Prioress in Real Life

Eileen Power

The Prioress who travels with her nun chaplain and three priests toward Canterbury cathedral in Chaucer's most famous work was modeled closely on a real prioress named Madame Eglentyne. As noted medieval historian Eileen Power, formerly of the University of London, points out in this excerpt from her well-known book *Medieval People*, scholars have shown that Chaucer's description of the character conforms perfectly in every detail with fourteenth-century English prioresses. This is strong evidence that Chaucer was, in Power's words, "one of the most wonderful observers in the whole of English literature." Power's informative and witty account of the life Eglentyne led behind the closed doors of her nunnery constitutes a colorful and useful companion piece for the portion of *The Canterbury Tales* devoted to her character.

Everyone knows Chaucer's description of the Prioress, Madame Eglentyne, who rode with that very motley and talkative company on the way to Canterbury. There is no portrait in his gallery which has given rise to more diverse comment among critics. One interprets it as a cutting attack on the worldliness of the Church; another thinks that Chaucer meant to draw a charming and sympathetic picture of womanly gentleness; one says that it is a caricature, another an ideal; and an American professor even finds in it a psychological study of thwarted maternal instinct, apparently because Madame Eglentyne was fond of little dogs and told a story about a schoolboy. The mere historian may be excused from following these vagaries. To him Chaucer's Prioress, like Chaucer's Monk and Chaucer's Friar, will sim-

From *Medieval People* by Eileen Power (London: Methuen, 1924). Reprinted by permission of Routledge, UK.

ply be one more instance of the almost photographic accuracy of the poet's observation. The rippling undercurrent of satire is always there; but it is Chaucer's own peculiar satire—mellow, amused, uncondemning, the most subtle kind of satire, which does not depend upon exaggeration. The literary critic has only Chaucer's words and his own heart, or sometimes (low be it spoken) his own desire to be original, by which to guide his judgement. But the historian knows; he has all sorts of historical sources in which to study nunneries, and there he meets Chaucer's Prioress at every turn. Above all, he has the bishops' registers.

PRICELESS TIDBITS FROM BISHOPS' REGISTERS

For a long time historians foolishly imagined that kings and wars and parliaments and the jury system alone were history; they liked chronicles and Acts of Parliament, and it did not strike them to go and look in dusty episcopal archives for the big books in which medieval bishops entered up the letters which they wrote and all the complicated business of running their dioceses. But when historians did think of looking there, they found a mine of priceless information about almost every side of social and ecclesiastical life. They had to dig for it of course, for almost all that is worth knowing has to be mined like precious metals out of a rock; and for one nugget the miner often has to grub for days underground in a mass of dullness; and when he has got it he has to grub in his own heart, or else he will not understand it. The historians found fine gold in the bishops' registers, when once they persuaded themselves that it was not beneath their dignity to grub there. They found descriptions of vicarages, with all their furniture and gardens; they found marriage disputes; they found wills full of entertaining legacies to people dead hundreds of years ago; they found excommunications; they found indulgences to men for relieving the poor, repairing roads, and building bridges, long before there was any poor law, or any county council; they found trials for heresy and witchcraft; they found accounts of miracles worked at the tombs of saints and even of some quite unsaintly people . . . ; they found lists of travelling expenses when the bishops rode round their dioceses. . . . Last, but not least, the historians found a multitude of documents about monasteries, and among these documents they found visitation records, and among visitation records they found

Chaucer's Prioress, smiling full simple and coy, fair forehead, well-pinched wimple, necklace, little dogs, and all, as
though she had stepped into a stuffy register by mistake for
the *Canterbury Tales* and was longing to get out again.

CHAUCER INTRODUCES THE PRIORESS

*Madame Eglentyne is the fourth character Chaucer intro-
duces in the General Prologue to* The Canterbury Tales,
excerpted here from Vincent F. Hopper's translation.

There was also a Nun, a PRIORESS,
That in her smiling was simple and sweet;
Her greatest oath was but by Saint Loy;[1]
And she was called Madame Eglentine.
Full well she sang the divine service,
Intoned in her nose full seemly;
And French she spoke fluently and elegantly,
After the school of Stratford-at-Bow,[2]
For Parisian French was to her unknown.
At meals well taught was she withal;
She let no morsel from her lips fall,
Nor wet her fingers deeply in her sauce.
Well could she handle a morsel, and be careful
That no drop ever fell upon her breast.
Courtesy was her particular delight.
Her upper lip wiped she so clean,
That in her cup was no trace seen
Of grease, when she had drunk her draught.
Becomingly after her food she reached,
And indeed she was very diverting,
And very pleasant, and amiable of disposition,
And she strove to simulate the behavior
Of court, and be stately in manner,
And to be held worthy of reverence.
But, to speak of her inner nature,
She was so charitable and so piteous,
She would weep, if only she saw a mouse
Caught in a trap, if it were dead or bleeding.
Some small dogs had she, that she fed
With roasted meat, or milk and finest bread.
But sorely would she weep if one of them were dead,
Of if men struck it with a stick smartly:
She was altogether kind and tender hearted.

1. an oath by Saint Loy was the mildest possible form of swearing
2. a nunnery near London

COMPLAINTS TO THE BISHOP

This was the reason that Madame Eglentyne got into the register. In the Middle Ages all the nunneries of England, and a great many of the monasteries, used to be visited at intervals by the bishop of their diocese—or by somebody sent by him—in order to see whether they were behaving properly. . . . First of all, he sent a letter to say he was coming, and to bid the nuns prepare for him. Then he came, with his clerks and a learned official or two, and was met solemnly by the prioress and all the nuns, and preached a sermon in their church, and was entertained, perhaps, to dinner. And then he prepared to examine them, and one by one they came before him, in order of rank, beginning with the prioress, and what they had to do was to tell tales about each other. He wanted to find out if the prioress were ruling well, and if the services were properly performed, and if the finances were in good order, and if discipline were maintained; and if any nun had a complaint, then was the time to make it.

And the nuns were full of complaints. A modern schoolgirl would go pale with horror over their capacity for talebearing. If one nun had boxed her sister's ears, if another had cut church, if another were too much given to entertaining friends, if another went out without a licence, if another had run away with a wandering fluteplayer, the bishop was sure to hear about it; that is, unless the whole convent were in a disorderly state, and the nuns had made a compact to wink at each other's peccadilloes; and not to betray them to the bishop, which occasionally happened. And if the prioress were at all unpopular he was quite certain to hear all about her. 'She fares splendidly in her own room and never invites us,' says one nun; 'She has favourites,' says another, 'and when she makes corrections she passes lightly over those whom she likes, and speedily punishes those whom she dislikes'; 'She is a fearful scold,' says a third; 'She dresses more like a secular person than a nun, and wears rings and necklaces,' says a fourth; 'She goes riding to see her friends far too often,' says a fifth; 'She-is-a-very-bad-business-woman-and-she-has-let-the-house-get-into-debt-and-the-church-is-falling-about-our-ears-and-we-don't-get-enough-food-and-she-hasn't-given-us-any-clothes-for-two-years-and-she-has-sold-woods-and-farms-without-your-licence-and-she-has-pawned-our-best-set-of-spoons; and no wonder, when she never consults us in any business as she ought to do.' They go on like that for pages, and the bishop must often have wanted to put his fingers in his ears and shout to them to stop; especially as the prioress had probably spent half an hour, for her part, in telling him how disobedient and ill-tempered, and thoroughly badly behaved the nuns were.

All these tales the bishop's clerk solemnly wrote down in a big book, and when the examination was over the bishop summoned all the nuns together again. And if they had answered 'All is well', as they sometimes did, or only mentioned trivial faults, he commended them and went his way; and if they had shown that things really were in a bad way, he investigated particular charges and scolded the culprits and ordered them to amend, and when he got back to his palace, or the manor where he was staying, he wrote out a set of injunctions, based on the complaints, and saying exactly how things were to be improved; and of these injunctions one copy was entered in his register and another was sent by hand to the nuns, who were supposed to read it aloud at intervals and to obey everything in it. We have in many bishops' registers these lists of injunctions, copied into them by the bishops' clerks, and in some, notably in a splendid fifteenth-century Lincoln register, belonging to the good bishop Alnwick, we have also the evidence of the nuns, just as it was taken down from their chattering mouths, and these are the most human and amusing of all medieval records. . . .

EGLENTYNE AS A NOVICE

Let us see what light the registers will throw upon Madame Eglentyne, before Chaucer observed her mounting her horse outside the Tabard Inn. Doubtless she first came to the nunnery when she was quite a little girl, because girls counted as grown up when they were fifteen in the Middle Ages; they could be married out of hand at twelve, and they could become nuns for ever at fourteen. Probably Eglentyne's father had three other daughters to marry, each with a dowry, and a gay young spark of a son, who spent a lot of money on fashionable suits. . . . So he thought he had better settle the youngest at once; and he got together a dowry (it was rarely possible to get into a nunnery without one, though Church law really forbade anything except voluntary offerings), and, taking Eglentyne by the hand one summer day, he popped her into a nunnery a few miles off, which had been founded by his ancestors. We may even know what it cost him; it was rather a select, aristocratic house, and he had to pay an entrance fee of £200 [200 English pounds] in modern money; and then he had to give Eglentyne her new habit and a bed, and some other furniture; and he had to make a feast on the day she became a nun, and invite all the nuns and all his own friends; and he had to tip the friar, who preached the sermon; and, altogether, it was a great affair. But the feast would not come at once, because Eglentyne would have to remain a novice for some years, until she was old enough to take the vows. So she would stay in the convent and be taught how to sing and to read, and to talk French ... with the other novices. Perhaps she was the youngest, for girls often did not enter the convent until they were old enough to decide for themselves whether they wanted to be nuns; but there were certainly some other quite tiny novices learning their lessons; and occasionally there would be a little girl like the one whose sad fate is recorded in a dull law-book, shut up in a nunnery by a wicked stepfather who wanted her inheritance (a nun could not inherit land, because she was supposed to be dead to the world), and told by the nuns that the devil would fly away with her if she tried to set foot outside the door. However, Eglentyne had a sunny disposition and liked life in the nunnery, and had a natural aptitude for the pretty table manners which she learnt there, as well as for talking French, and though she was not at all prim and liked the gay clothes and pet dogs which she used to see at home in her mother's bower, still she had no hesitation at all about taking the veil when she was fifteen, and indeed she rather liked the fuss that was made of her, and being called *Madame* or *Dame*, which was the courtesy title always given to a nun.

A NUN'S DAILY ROUTINE

The years passed and Eglentyne's life jogged along peacefully enough behind the convent walls. The great purpose for which the nunneries existed, and which most of them fulfilled not unworthily, was the praise of God. Eglentyne spent a great deal of her time singing and praying in the convent church.... The nuns had seven monastic offices [prayer services] to say every day. About 2 A.M. the night office was said; they all got out of bed when the bell rang, and went down in the cold and the dark to the church choir and said Matins, followed immediately by Lauds. Then they went back to bed, just as the dawn was breaking in the sky, and slept again for three hours, and then got up for good at six o'clock and said Prime.... They had in all about eight hours' sleep, broken in the middle by the night service. They had three meals, a light repast of bread and beer after prime in the morning, a solid dinner to the accompaniment of reading aloud in the middle of the day, and a short supper immediately after vespers at 5 or 6 P.M.

From 12 to 5 P.M. in winter and from 1 to 6 P.M. in summer Eglentyne and her sisters were supposed to devote themselves to manual or brain work, interspersed with a certain amount of sober and godly recreation. She would spin, or embroider vestments with the crowned monogram *M* of the Blessed Virgin in blue and gold thread, or make little silken purses for her friends and finely sewn bands for them to bind round their arms after a bleeding.... In the summer Eglentyne was sometimes allowed to work in the convent garden, or even to go out haymaking with the other nuns....

Except for certain periods of relaxation strict silence was supposed to be observed in the convent for a large part of the day, and if Eglentyne desired to communicate with her sisters, she was urged to do so by means of signs. The persons who drew up the lists of signs which were in use in medieval monastic houses, however, combined a preternatural ingenuity with an extremely exiguous sense of humour, and the sort of dumb pandemonium which went on at Eglentyne's dinner table must often have been more mirthprovoking than speech. The sister who desired fish would 'wag her hands displayed sidelings in manner of a fish tail'; she who wanted milk would 'draw her left little finger in manner of milking'; for mustard one would 'hold her nose in the upper part of her right fist and rub it'; another for salt would 'fillip with her right thumb and forefinger over the left thumb'; another desirous of wine would 'move her forefinger up and down the end of her thumb afore her eye'; and the guilty sacristan, struck by the thought that she had not provided incense for the Mass, would 'put her two fingers into her nostrils'. In one such table drawn up for nuns there are no less than 106 signs, and on the whole it is not surprising that the rule of the same nuns enjoins that 'it is never lawful to use them without some reason and profitable need, for oft-times more hurt hath an evil word, and more offence it may be to God'.

Bored, Lazy, and Scandalous

The nuns, of course, would not have been human if they had not sometimes grown a little weary of all these services and this silence; for the religious life was not, nor was it intended to be, an easy one. It was not a mere means of escape from work and responsibility. In the early golden age of monasticism only men and women with a vocation, that is to say a real genius for monastic life, entered convents. Moreover, when there they worked very hard with hand and brain, as well as with soul, and so they got variety of occupation, which is as good as a holiday.... Thus monks and nuns did not find the services monotonous, and indeed regarded them as by far the best part of the day. But in the later Middle Ages, when Chaucer lived, young people had begun to enter monastic houses rather as a profession than as a vocation. Many truly spiritual men and women still took the vows, but with them came others who were little suited to monastic life, and who lowered its standard, because it was hard and uncongenial to them. Eglentyne became a nun because her father did not want the trouble and expense of finding her a husband, and because being a nun was about the only career for a well-born lady who did not marry. Moreover, by this time, monks and nuns had grown more lazy, and did little work with their hands and still less with their heads, particularly in nunneries, where the early tradition of learning had died out and where many nuns could hardly understand the Latin in which their services were written. The result was that monastic life began to lose that essential variety which St Benedict had designed for it, and as a result the regularity sometimes became irksome, and the series of services degenerated into a mere routine of peculiar monotony, which many of the singers could no longer keep alive with spiritual fervour. Thus sometimes ... the services became empty forms, to be hurried through with scant devotion and occasionally with scandalous irreverence. It was the almost inevitable reaction from too much routine.

Carelessness in the performance of the monastic hours was an exceedingly common fault during the later Middle Ages, though the monks were always worse about it than the nuns. Sometimes they 'cut' the services. Sometimes they be-haved with the utmost levity, as at Exeter [in southwestern England] in 1330, where the canons giggled and joked and quarrelled during the services and dropped hot candle wax from the upper stalls on to the shaven heads of the singers in the stalls below! Sometimes they came late to matins, in the small hours after midnight. This fault was common in nunneries, for the nuns always would insist on having pri-vate drinkings and gossipings in the evening after compline [an early-evening prayer service] instead of going straight to bed, as the rule demanded—a habit which did not conduce to wakefulness at 1 A.M. . . . At the nunnery of Stainfield in 1519 the bishop discovered that half an hour sometimes elapsed between the last stroke of the bell and the beginning of the service, and that some of the nuns did not sing, but dozed, partly because they had not enough candles, but chiefly because they went late to bed; and whoever is with-out sin among us, let him cast the first stone! There was a tendency also among both monks and nuns to slip out be-fore the end of the service on any good or bad excuse: they had to see after the dinner or the guest-house, their gardens needed weeding, or they did not feel well. But the most com-mon fault of all was to gabble through the services as quickly as they could in order to get them over. They left out the syllables at the beginning and end of words, they omit-ted the dipsalma or pause between two verses, so that one side of the choir was beginning the second half before the other side had finished the first. . . .

A Good-Natured Autocrat

But we must be back at Eglentyne. She went on living for ten or twelve years as a simple nun, and she sang the services very nicely and had a sweet temper and pretty manners and was very popular. Moreover, she was of good birth; Chaucer tells us a great deal about her beautiful behaviour at table and her courtesy, which shows that she was a lady born and bred; indeed, his description of this might have been taken straight out of one of the feudal books of deportment for girls; even her personal beauty—straight nose, grey eyes, and little red mouth—conforms to the courtly standard. The convents were apt to be rather snobbish; ladies and rich burgesses' daughters got into them, but poor and low-born girls never. So the nuns probably said to each other that what with her pretty ways and her good temper and her aristocratic connexions, wouldn't it be a good thing to choose her for prioress when the old prioress died? And so they did, and she had been a prioress for some years when Chaucer met her. At first it was very exciting, and Eglentyne liked being called 'Mother' by nuns who were older than herself, and having a private room to sit in and all the visitors to entertain. But she soon found that it was not by any means all a bed of roses; for there was a great deal of business to be done by the head of a house—not only looking after the internal discipline of the convent, but also superintending money matters and giving orders to the bailiffs on her estates, and seeing that the farms were paying well, and the tithes coming in to the churches which belonged to the nunnery, and that the Italian merchants who came to buy the wool off her sheep's backs gave a good price for it. In all this business she was supposed to take the advice of the nuns, meeting in the chapter-house, where all business was transacted. I am afraid that sometimes Eglentyne used to think that it was much better to do things by herself, and so she would seal documents with the convent seal without telling them. One should always distrust the head of an office or school or society who says, with a self-satisfied air, that it is much more satisfactory to do the thing herself than to depute it to the proper subordinates; it either means that she is an autocrat, or else that she cannot organize. Madame Eglentyne was rather an autocrat, in a good-natured sort of way, and besides she hated bother. So she did not always consult the nuns; and I fear too (after many researches into that past of hers which Chaucer forgot to mention) that she often tried to evade rendering an account of income and expenditure to them every year, as she was supposed to do.

The nuns, of course, objected to this; and the first time the bishop came on his rounds they complained about it to him. They said, too, that she was a bad business woman and got into debt; and that when she was short of money she used to sell woods belonging to the convent, and promise annual pensions to various people in return for lump sums down, and lease out farms for a long time at low rates, and do various other things by which the convent would lose in the long run. And besides, she had let the roof of the church get into such ill repair that rain came through the holes on to their heads when they were singing; and would my lord bishop please to look at the holes in their clothes and tell her to provide them with new ones? Other wicked prioresses used sometimes even to pawn the plate and jewels of the convent, to get money for their own private purposes. But Eglentyne was not at all wicked or dishonest, though she was a bad manager; the fact was that she had no head for figures. I am *sure* that she had no head for figures; you have only got to read Chaucer's description of her to know that she was not a mathematician. Besides the nuns were exaggerating: their clothes were not in holes, only just a little threadbare. Madame Eglentyne was far too fastidious to allow ragged clothes about her; and as to the roof of the church, she had meant to save enough money to have some tiles put on to it, but it really *was* very hard to make two ends meet in a medieval nunnery, especially if (as I repeat) you had no head for figures. . . .

How She Became Worldly

Eglentyne, it seems, was never really interested in business, and was quite pleased to have her time taken up with looking after internal affairs and entertaining visitors, with an occasional jaunt outside to see how the estates were getting on. And she began to find that she could lead a much freer and gayer life now that she was a prioress; for the prioress of a convent had rooms of her own, instead of sharing the common dormitory and refectory; sometimes she even had a sort of little house with a private kitchen. . . . A superior generally had with her one nun to act as her companion and assist her in the choir and be a witness to her good behaviour; this nun was called her chaplain, and was supposed to be changed every year, to prevent favouritism. It will be remembered that when Madame Eglentyne went on her pilgrimage she took her nun chaplain with her, as well as three priests; that was because no nun was ever allowed to go out alone. One of Madame Eglentyne's duties as prioress was to entertain visitors with her celebrated cheer of court, and we may be sure that she had a great many. . . .

She probably became more worldly as time went on, because she had so many opportunities for social intercourse. Not only had she to entertain visitors in the convent, but often the business of the house took her away upon journeys and these offered many opportunities for hobnobbing with her neighbours. Sometimes she had to go to London to see after a law-suit and that was a great excursion with another nun, or perhaps two, and a priest and several yeomen to look after her. Sometimes she had to go and see the bishop, to get permission to take in some little schoolgirls. Sometimes she went to the funeral of a great man, whom her father knew and who left her twenty shillings and a silver cup in his will. Sometimes she went to the wedding of one of her sisters, or to be godmother to their babies; though the bishops did not like these worldly ties, or the dances and merry-makings which accompanied weddings and christenings. Indeed her nuns occasionally complained about her journeys and said that though she pretended it was all on the business of the house, they had their doubts; and would the bishop please just look into it. . . .

This then was Chaucer's Prioress in real life, for the poet who drew her was one of the most wonderful observers in the whole of English literature. We may wade through hundreds of visitation reports and injunctions and everywhere the grey eyes of his Prioress will twinkle at us out of their pages, and in the end we must always go to Chaucer for her picture, to sum up everything that historical records have taught us. As the bishop found her, so he saw her, aristocratic, tender-hearted, worldly . . . liking pretty clothes and little dogs; a lady of importance, attended by a nun and three priests. . . . So we take our leave of her, characteristically on the road to Canterbury.

The Churlish Miller's Vulgar Tale

Margaret Hallissy

In this excerpt from her book *A Companion to Chaucer's Canterbury Tales*, Chaucerian scholar Margaret Hallissy, professor of English at Long Island University, describes the characters and plot of the *Miller's Tale*. As she explains, these stereotypical character types and comic plot twists are typical of the fabliau, a short anecdote usually containing slapstick humor and sexually explicit jokes and situations that was very popular in the Middle Ages. Hallissy makes the point that Chaucer's medieval readers fully expected a lowborn, ill-bred fellow like the Miller to tell such a vulgar tale.

Like the "Knight's Tale" which precedes it, the "Miller's Tale" is a story of the competition between men in love with the same woman—but with a difference. But where the "Knight's Tale" is a romance, the "Miller's Tale" belongs to an equally popular but different medieval genre, the *fabliau*. The audience has been warned in the linking passage that it should come as no surprise that the Miller, a "churl," or low, vulgar character, would tell a "churl's tale." The *fabliau*, or churl's tale, is the medieval equivalent of the dirty joke. The characters, being of low *estat*, are motivated by the basest possible drives. Love for the *fabliau* character is a matter not of the heart, mind, and spirit as it is in the romance, but of the body only. Appropriately, then, the tale is told in the low style; vulgarity abounds, and the modern audience becomes well acquainted with the medieval version of common four-letter words for the most basic of human functions.

ANTICIPATING THE ADULTERY TO COME

Parallel to the angelic Emelye in the "Knight's Tale" is the earthy Alisoun, no virgin like Emelye but the eighteen-year-

From *A Companion to Chaucer's "Canterbury Tales"* by Margaret Hallissy. Copyright ©1995 by Margaret Hallissy. Reproduced by permission of Greenwood Publishing Group, Inc., Westport, Conn.

old wife of the aged John, a carpenter of Oxford. To medieval people, the idea of an old man marrying a young girl was wildly funny. Such a man deceives himself, they thought, about his own ability to satisfy a young girl; it is a foregone conclusion that his frustrated wife will one day betray him with a younger and more virile man. (This situation arises again in the "Merchant's Tale.") Immediately, the medieval audience would expect sexual complications simply from the fact that foolish John has taken in a "poor scholar," a student at Oxford University, as a boarder in his house.

Oxford is now and was then a university town. The "town," or local residents, often found itself at odds with the "gown," the university students (who wore as symbol of their calling the academic robes familiar today as graduation garb). Unlike Chaucer's Oxford Clerk, a dedicated scholar, many students saw university life as a prime opportunity to misbehave and considered the women of the town as fair game for seduction. Nicholas the poor scholar is typical of such students. His prime study is astrology, considered a science in the Middle Ages; in his room he keeps the *Almagest*, a famed astrological treatise, other "books great and small," and assorted tools of the astrologer's art. But his main interest is nonacademic: "secret love and . . . pleasure." How foolish John the carpenter is to rent a room to such a young man—especially since John has a voluptuous young wife.

The common literary motif of the old man in love with the young woman is called by a Latin name: the *senex amans*, the old man in love. John is a typical example of that stereotype:

This carpenter had newly wed a wife,
Whom he loved more than his life;
She was eighteen years of age.
He was jealous, and held her tight in cage,
For she was wild and young, and he was old
And deemed himself likely to become a cuckold.

The cuckold, the husband whose wife had been unfaithful, was believed to wear on his head a set of horns visible to everyone but him. The betrayal of a jealous *senex amans* like John provided material for a stock *fabliau* plot, a plot so common that, even this early in the story, the medieval audience would gleefully anticipate the predictable outcome. Audience anticipation of the adultery to come is reinforced by the Miller's long and appreciative description of Alisoun's appealing features: her clothes, her face, her body, even the scent of her breath. Alisoun, in short, is adorable, like a little flower. She would be just right for a lord to bed or a yeoman to wed. Notice the distinctions of *estat:* an upper-class man would not have to marry her, but a lower-class man would.

Since John the carpenter has indeed married her, she should be faithful to him; but implicit in the *senex amans* motif is the assumption that Alisoun is sexually unsatisfied and thus easily seducible by a younger and more virile man—a man just like Nicholas. How foolish of John to leave the two at home alone while he goes to Osney! The husband out of the way, Nicholas quickly makes his move... and begs her to satisfy him....

She makes a perfunctory attempt at refusal:

> And with her head she quickly twisted away,
> And said, "I will not kiss thee, by my faith!
> Why, let be," said she. "Let be, Nicholas!
> Or I will cry 'out, harrow, and alas!'
> Remove your hands, for your courtesy!"

Were she to cry out, her neighbors might think she was being raped, for "raising the hue and cry" was a key element in proving resistance under medieval English rape law. But it rapidly becomes clear that Alisoun consents to Nicholas's advances. So swift is this courtship that it is clear that Alisoun is a woman of exceedingly flexible moral standards—she is, in modern terms, easy. She promptly agrees to have sex with Nicholas as soon as it can be arranged. No problem, Nicholas assures her: students are smarter than carpenters any day. And so they agree to deceive Alisoun's jealous husband.

AN ELABORATE HOAX

The rest of the *fabliau* involves an elaborate plot to get the couple together in the absence of John. To add complexity to the predictable situation, Chaucer adds yet another plot and introduces a new character, the parish clerk Absolon. Not a priest in holy orders but an unordained deacon (comparable to an altar server today), the parish clerk assists at liturgical ceremonies, for example, by wielding the censer, or incense burner, on the holidays. In the course of these clerical duties, he falls in lust with the carpenter's wife:

> I dare well say, if she had been a mouse,
> And he a cat, he would have pounced immediately.

Absolon has several other functions appropriate to his status as a learned, or at least literate, man; he does barbering and bloodletting; he draws up legal documents; he sings and plays musical instruments. His music and singing shape his self-image in that he sees himself as a courtly lover, serenading his lady in hopes to win her love.

MEDIEVAL PRACTICAL JOKES

In his well-known Reader's Encyclopedia, *scholar William R. Benét gives this description of the* fabliau.

[The *fabliaux* were] short humorous tales, often ribald or scurrilous. Highly popular in the Middle Ages, they are situation comedies burlesquing the weaknesses of human nature; women, priests, and gullible fools are often the butts of the buffoonery, which sometimes becomes savagely bitter. The material derives from the oral folk tradition of bawdy anecdotes, practical jokes, and clever tricks of revenge, but the term *fabliau* was first specifically applied to a medieval French literary form, a narrative of three hundred to four hundred lines in octosyllabic couplets. About 150 of these are still extant. Similar prose tales became popular all over Europe, as in Boccaccio's *Decameron.* Apparently only a few narratives in the style of the *fabliau* were written in England; the most notable are the ones Chaucer included in his *Canterbury Tales,* such as the tales told by the Miller, the Reeve, the Friar, the Summoner, and the Shipman.

But Alisoun is no lady, courtly or otherwise. Having just heard the "Knight's Tale," the Canterbury pilgrims know how foolish Absolon is for treating Alisoun as if she were Emelye. Standing beneath his lady's window, he plays his cithern (a stringed instrument) and sings love songs. Foolish also is John, who, deaf to events taking place right in his household, hears Absolon but doesn't understand what his singing means. Absolon's courtship goes on, with Absolon assuming all the poses of the courtly lover (more music, sleepless nights, gifts) and Alisoun ignoring him because "she loves so this pleasant Nicholas."

Nicholas soon has an opportunity to prove how pleasant he is when John makes another trip to Osney. It would seem that this provides the lovers with the opportunity they need; but Osney is apparently too short a trip for Nicholas to have the desired full night of love. Besides, in accordance with the popular town-versus-gown motif, the whole business will be more fun if the student can "beguile" the carpenter. So

Nicholas uses the Osney trip to plan an elaborate hoax.

As was mentioned at the beginning of the tale, Nicholas is a student of astrology. Since all university subjects look mysterious to the uneducated, Nicholas can easily use his alleged learning to beguile John. Nicholas begins by staying in his room for such an unnaturally long time that John knocks on his door to find out if anything is wrong. When Nicholas does not respond, John peeks in through a small aperture in the door made for the cat to come and go. He sees Nicholas sitting, "gaping upwards, / As if he had gazed upon the new moon," that is, as if he had gone mad. John is shocked and attributes Nicholas's deranged state to an excess of learning:

> This man is fallen, with his astronomy,
> Into some madness or some agony.
> I always thought that it should be!
> Men should not know of God's privacy.
> Yes, blessed be always an unlearned man
> Who knows nothing but his belief!

The anti-intellectual's credo is as John states it: the less known, the better; all knowledge is a violation of "God's privacy"; study leads to madness.

But as the audience knows, Nicholas is perfectly sane. He confides to John the alleged result of his astrological studies: a flood is coming, worse than Noah's, and the only way their little household can survive is for each to spend a night in three separate large buckets, "kneading-tubs," tied to the roof-beams. When the floodwaters rise, they can cut the cords and float away.... While John is in his tub, obediently waiting for the deluge, Nicholas and Alisoun will climb down from their respective lofty perches and have the long-awaited night of love....

EXPLOITING THE BASEST INSTINCTS

It seems that Nicholas and Alisoun will finally get their undisturbed night of love. But since John the carpenter has not appeared in public lately, the third lover, Absolon, assumes that John has made yet another trip to Osney. He, too, sees this as his chance to woo the carpenter's wife....

John is in his kneading-tub, Alisoun and Nicholas are in bed. Having prepared himself for the anticipated kiss by "chewing grain and licorice, / To smell sweet"—using the medieval equivalent of breath-mints—Absolon goes to Alisoun's window and begins his serenade:

Awake, my lover, and speak to me!
Little do you think upon my woe,
That for your love I sweat where'er I go. . . .
It's true, my love, I have such love-longing
That like a turtle-dove's is my mourning.
I cannot eat more than does a maid.

The high-style language is right out of the courtly love tradition. But unladylike Alisoun is annoyed, and wants only to
get rid of her pesty courtier and get back into bed with
Nicholas. . . .

Absolon refuses to leave without the kiss for which his
heart longs. Alisoun asks if he will go away once he gets his
kiss. "Yes, certainly, my love," Absolon replies. "Then get
ready," says she, "Here I come." And so occurs the climactic
event. In the darkness of the night, Absolon does not realize
that Alisoun has presented her posterior. The audience was
warned that this was a churl's tale, and so it is. But the low
and bawdy humor traditional in the *fabliau* requires that the
basest instincts be exploited to the full; and so the kiss is not
the last of the tale's vulgarisms.

Earlier, when Absolon was introduced, the audience was
informed that he was "somewhat squeamish / Of farting."
Apparently an irrelevant detail then, Absolon's squeamish-
ness is now essential to the plot. Having kissed Alisoun's
nether regions, an act still deemed insulting today . . . he is
intent only on revenge. So he concocts a plot of his own. He
gets a hot branding iron from a blacksmith and returns to
the infamous window to beg for another kiss.

This situation arouses Nicholas's competitiveness with
Absolon. As was obvious before, when Nicholas bypassed a
simple opportunity in favor of the more ambitious plot to
"beguile" John the carpenter, much of Nicholas's pleasure
in Alisoun depends on outwitting other men also in love
with her. . . . So now, Nicholas, awake . . . decides that the
next step should be that Absolon "should kiss his ass ere he
escape." When Absolon comes to the window for Alisoun's
kiss, Nicholas places his naked posterior out that same very
active window. Not contented with this expression of contempt, Nicholas further insults the squeamish Absolon:

This Nicholas anon let fly a fart
As great as if it were a thunderclap.

Though revolted, Absolon is ready:

with his iron hot,

And he smote Nicholas upon the ass.
Off goes the skin a hand-breadth about!
The hot branding-iron so burned his buttocks,
That for the pain he thought that he would die.

At this climactic moment, Chaucer's careful planning becomes apparent. Scalded, Nicholas screams: "Help! Water! Water!" The sleeping John, hanging in his kneading-tub, hears the cry and, assuming that Noah's flood has come again, does as he was told. He cuts the cord which ties his tub to the rafters, and, with no deluge beneath him, down he falls to the floor. . . .

A LIGHT-HEARTED WORLD

Idealistic devotion, noble rivalry, and mutual respect, as demonstrated by Palamon and Arcite in the "Knight's Tale," are replaced in the "Miller's Tale" by lechery and vulgar competitiveness between Nicholas and Absolon, and the uxorious foolishness of John. Alisoun, readily available to her handy young boarder, is the more sluttish when compared to the virginal Emelye, reward for male valor but only within holy matrimony. Although all the characters in the "Miller's Tale" have sinned in their own way, no one has suffered severely, no one dies: the *fabliau* world is a light-hearted world in which sex without love has no serious consequences. As in the "Knight's Tale," characters fall from fortune (most noticeably John, from his foolish perch in the rafters); but since neither they nor their peccadilloes are really of cosmic importance, their misadventures are matter for comedy. Like the appreciative Canterbury pilgrims, the modern audience laughs at the foolishness of men governed by their appetites for a girl as sweet as apples, as pretty as a flower.

The Moral of the *Nun's Priest's Tale*

Saul N. Brody

On the surface, the Nun's Priest's story about a nearly fatal encounter between a rooster and fox is a charming and seemingly simple tale. However, as Saul N. Brody, a professor of English at City University of New York, points out, Chaucer uses this simple format to examine a more intricate concept, one he explores elsewhere in *The Canterbury Tales*. This is the idea that in all fiction there is an element of truth. In this case, Chaucer presents a clearly unrealistic premise—talking barnyard animals—but gives these creatures human qualities and has them comment on the truth of the human condition. This makes the tale, as in a similar modern example of barnyard allegory, George Orwell's *Animal Farm*, a clever blend of fiction and truth.

Readers of the *Nun's Priest's Tale* must be struck by the simplicity of the plot. A rooster in a barnyard has what he takes to be a prophetic dream in which a hound-like beast enters the yard. One of his hens hears him groaning, and after she wakens him, they engage in a debate over whether or not the dream is a forecast of things to come. However, in spite of his own argument that the dream is prophetic, the rooster is so taken with the hen's beauty that he disregards the dream's warning altogether. Thus, upon entering the barnyard, the fox is easily able to flatter and seize the rooster. Nevertheless, through an appeal to the fox's pride, the rooster outsmarts and escapes from him.

All this is narrated in an unhurried, considered fashion. Everything is detailed and made plain. There is room and time to introduce the dairywoman who owns the rooster; to describe Chaunticleer's colors; to allow the chickens to

From Saul N. Brody, "Truth and Fiction in the Nun's Priest's Tale," *Chaucer Review*, vol. 14, no. 1, 1979, 33-47. Copyright 1979 by The Pennsylvania State University. Reproduced by permission of the Pennsylvania State University Press.

argue at length about dreams in direct discourse; to describe the tumult on the farm as the fox is pursued. The fanciful life of the barnyard comes alive through elaborate description and faithfully rendered conversation, so that finally everything seems exact—not merely the setting, but even the colors of the animals and their feelings.

CHAUNTICLEER'S DREAM

Here, from the J.U. Nicolson translation of The Canterbury Tales, *Chaucer's famous rooster speaks.*

So it befell that, in a bright dawning,
As Chanticleer 'midst wives and sisters all
Sat on his perch, the which was on the hall,
And next him sat the winsome Pertelote,
This Chanticleer he groaned within his throat
Like man that in his dreams is troubled sore.
And when fair Pertelote thus heard him roar,
She was aghast and said: "O sweetheart dear,
What ails you that you groan so? Do you hear?
You are a sleepy herald. Fie, for shame!"
    And he replied to her thus: "Ah, *madame*,
I pray you that you take it not in grief:
By God, I dreamed I'd come to such mischief,
Just now, my heart yet jumps with sore affright
Now God," cried he, "my vision read aright
And keep my body out of foul prison!
I dreamed, that while I wandered up and down
Within our yard, I saw there a strange beast
Was like a dog, and he'd have made a feast
Upon my body, and have had me dead.
His color yellow was and somewhat red;
And tipped his tail was, as were both his ears,
With black, unlike the rest, as it appears;
His snout was small and gleaming was each eye.
Remembering how he looked, almost I die;
And all this caused my groaning, I confess."

The story is so simple, and it is told with such precision, that the narrator could almost be taken to have witnessed the events he describes. Were it not that the tale is about speaking chickens in a barnyard, we might be tempted to call it realistic. But of course an obvious fact about the tale is that although the Nun's Priest presents it as something true and reasonable, he also makes it whimsical, extravagant, and unrealistic. His tale is thus paradoxically both absurd and serious, realistic and unrealistic, fictive and true, and that paradox, that tension between the literature-like and the life-like, is central to the tale. It is the source at once of much of its humor and much of its point, for through it the Nun's Priest asserts the ultimate seriousness not simply of his fiction, but of all fiction.

INTO THE ROOSTER'S REALM

The passage that opens the tale, in which the Nun's Priest introduces the widow and her farm and chickens, is shaped to emphasize the linking of fiction and truth in the narrative. The description of the old woman stresses her reality, the conditions of her life. In a few lines, we learn about her advanced age; her cottage . . . her three sows and three cows; her one sheep, named Malle; her diet; the fact that as a consequence she suffers from neither gout nor apoplexy; and her patient acceptance of her humble life. In all this, the Nun's Priest may be offering implicit comment on such women as the Prioress and the Wife of Bath, but he is also preparing us for the chickens, who are more the subject of the story than the widow who owns them. In fact, it is precisely through the contrast between the chickens and their owner that the narrator reminds us that he is telling a tale and we are listening to it.

The introductory description of Chaunticleer [the rooster] and Pertelote [the hen] begins with the same objective concentration on reality that marks the introduction of the widow. . . . But by the end of the passage, the teller has left the widow's prosaic world far behind, and entered into the poetic realm of a splendid rooster who not only can tell time perfectly, but who also is surrounded by a courtly harem of hens. . . . The Nun's Priest's performance is magnificent, capable, I think of seducing some of us into accepting the absurd reality of the chickens, or at least of not critically questioning it. And the narrator makes it seem as if that is exactly what he wants. At just the point where he tells us that his chickens sing lyrics, he interrupts his narrative to point out that it is not fictive, but historically reliable. . . . Of course, his actual (if implicit) assertion is that we are hearing a story, not objective truth, and naturally that assertion is exactly the one the narrator wants us to catch.

The Nun's Priest's device is traditional and simple. By dissolving dramatic illusion, he forces us to a heightened awareness of the tale as a work of fiction, as art and not reality itself. Significantly, each time he interrupts himself, he does the same thing, and he does it often enough and in such a way as to suggest that he is asking the audience to consider the implications not only of his storytelling, but also of storytelling itself. . . .

PARALLELS BETWEEN CHICKENS AND PEOPLE

The Nun's Priest prepares us for what is to follow by giving his chickens human qualities, something he does in fact throughout the tale, presumably not only for comic effect, for the sake of absurdity, but also to keep us aware of the story's implications for human beings. Consider the number of times and ways the Nun's Priest explicitly establishes parallels between chickens and people. In his first aside, he explains that at the time of Chaunticleer, beasts and birds could speak and sing. Later, while dreaming, Chaunticleer groans like a man vexed. Pertelote challenges him by demanding whether, having a beard, he also has the heart of a man. Chaunticleer later says that he would give his shirt to have Pertelote read the legend of Kenelm [a human fable], and later still the Nun's Priest quotes Chaunticleer's remarks on the baneful advice of women—women, not hens. He compares Chaunticleer's terror to a man's. The fox tells the rooster that he never heard a man sing as Chaunticleer's father did, and when Chaunticleer tries to outsing his father, he spreads his wings like a man who could not see his betrayal. . . . Whatever else these passages may do, they all serve the same purpose as the Nun's Priest's interruptions of his story, that is, they compel us to take a critical view of it, to focus on the story's implications for human beings. And the result is that by absurdly comparing chickens to people, the Nun's Priest keeps us from holding illusions about either. Chaunticleer may be as royal as a prince, but he is in his yard, every moment the cock, and every moment the embodiment of foolish masculine pride and arrogance. . . .

It is through this humanizing . . . that the narrator sets us up for his prediction of the coming disaster and his observation on the transcience of worldly joy. The language echoes the Monk's earlier remarks on the nature of tragedy, the catastrophes that befall men, and the Nun's Priest emphasizes the truth of the axiom that *worldly joye is soone ago* by suggesting that if a rhetorician knew how, he might enter it in a chronicle. . . . Thus, by interrupting the narrative, the Nun's Priest reminds us that it is a work of fiction about a laughable cock who perhaps ought in one light to be taken seriously, for the bird is about to experience a virtually human catastrophe in a virtually human way. . . .

SEARCHING FOR THE STORY'S MORAL

There are . . . three major digressions in the tale, and they all point to the presence of truth in the Nun's Priest's fiction. The first ends with the suggestion that stories, including the Nun's Priest's own, can mirror human passions accurately and thereby influence human behavior, or at least perceptions of the human condition; the second indicates that even a comic story about animals can echo human catastrophes and raise the sorts of questions that human catastrophes do, questions about the influences of women and predestination, for example; and the third digression, with its string of comically deflating mock-heroic passages, once again implicitly brings forward the parallel between the tale's animal world and the world of men. Taken together, then, the narrator's digressions and asides carefully pave the way for his closing reminder that although the tale may be a *folye* [folly] it contains truth:

> But ye that holden this tale a folye,
> As of a fox, or of a cok and hen,
> Taketh the moralite, goode men.

Of course, exactly what the *moralite* [moral] is has never been generally agreed upon. Some find it among the moral statements that end the narrative: Chaunticleer's warning against blindness to flattery, the fox's against speaking when it is better to be quiet, and the narrator's against heedlessness, negligence, and flattery. Others find it in various lessons implicit in the text, such as warnings against lechery or against human failings revealed through allegorical interpretation. And still others, recognizing the comic bent of the tale and finding a precise moral absent, caution against taking the tale too seriously, or pinpointing its lesson too precisely, or finding a lesson at all. Indeed, in the face of the varied lessons that have been discovered on and beneath the surface of the Nun's Priest's narrative—and rejected—a safe course would appear to be to avoid defining *the* lesson at all. On the other hand, the very presence of besetting ambiguity in the tale may indicate that if the work does contain a moral, that moral has to do with ambiguity itself—and most particularly with the ambiguity surrounding what is true and not true in the tale. . . .

Chaunticleer is, no doubt, the embodiment not simply of that problem but also of the larger uncertainty in the tale over what is true and not true generally. Though a rooster who scratches for corn, he is nevertheless capable of speaking, and what is more, of speaking truth, the truth about dreams, a truth he demonstrates by recourse to stories. A fantastical talking rooster, he appears in the middle of a piece of fiction that poses as truth, tells a series of *exempla* drawn largely (though not entirely) from authoritative sources, and then ignores the truth contained in them. The consequence is that he suffers a reversal of fortune, leading the narrator to remark that the story is as true as the story of Lancelot, itself an acknowledged piece of fiction. Like his story, Chaunticleer himself has a dual nature. He is true and fictive, rational and irrational, magnificent and trivial, human and animal.

Accordingly, when he moralizes on what has happened to him, he draws a lesson that is not so straightforwardly moral as it seems. Chaunticleer warns against being blind, presumably to flattery, but it is only by using flattery that he manages to escape from the fox; hence, while he does seem to have come to a realization about the danger of pride, he has been able to survive only by appealing to pride in someone else. Moreover, the lessons drawn by the fox and the narrator are similarly ambiguous. Although the fox warns against speaking foolishly, one can only suppose that if he again had the opportunity to capture and eat Chaunticleer, he would do so. And while the narrator's warning against heedlessness and flattery is morally sound from one point of view, from another and more cynical one it can be taken as a recommendation to villains (such as the fox) to keep their own interests firmly in view. In brief, all the lessons drawn at the close of the story are ambiguous, and for the very good reason that the human heart is ambiguous.

THE ELUSIVENESS OF TRUTH

What then is the point of the *Nun's Priest's Tale*? I take it that the story is about the complexity of things, about the elusiveness of truth and the need to pursue it. It does not really matter whether Chaunticleer's downfall is brought about by his lechery, his wife's advice, his susceptibility to flattery, his recklessness, or unknowable influences such as destiny. The heart of the matter is that Chaunticleer has a rational side that could have protected him, and he ought to have known better than to ignore it. At the end, perched in the tree, he sees that his survival will depend on his alertness in the future, his use of his higher faculties. Of course, his lower, his animal impulses, will always be ready to do him in, and that is his problem, as (the Nun's Priest would say) it is everyone's problem.

In short, one apparent truth about the tale is that it will not easily support one meaning, and if it is confused and ambiguous, if its moral is elusive, if it can be seen from a variety of angles, that is because the tale is less about a particular moral in it than about the very existence of moral possibilities. Accordingly, I suggest that the tale's lesson, its *fruyt*, is not to avoid, say, flattery, but to recognize that difficult moral choices are everywhere. The narrator, in raising all sorts of possibilities of meaning, compels the audience to confront the ambiguities raised in the tale, and he thus creates in his fiction a mirror of what individuals regularly confront in life. What moral meaning they extract from or impose upon life, or the story, presumably depends upon their ethical predispositions, and their burden is to make the right choices. . . .

The Nun's Priest is saying that any story . . . can be seen to have moral implications, not only stories told by a monk, but even an absurd piece of fiction by a priest about a cock, or an *exemplum* offered by that cock within the tale. To sharpen our perception of his own tale, he makes it altogether impossible to suspend disbelief. He frequently and consciously calls attention to himself as a story teller and to the poem as a story . . . [and also uses] comparisons between chickens and people, stories within his story, allusions to other stories, and parodies of literary styles. By doing all these things, the Nun's Priest compels us to focus on the mechanics of his art, on his tale as a consciously wrought work of fiction.

It is inviting to speculate that he does this because he is on a pilgrimage whose unifying activity is storytelling. His tale is in one light a comment on that activity, a suggestion that even if the pilgrimage's storytellers do not see it, their fictions are full of moral implications, of hidden truths, and he is thus reminding his listeners to be on the lookout for them. Those truths may not be clearly discernible, or their seriousness may be or may seem to be subverted by comic possibilities, but as in the case of Chaunticleer, the very salvation of the pilgrims may depend upon their ability to interpret what they hear.

The "Blockhead" Pilgrim Chaucer and His Two Tales

Trevor Whittock

At one point in *The Canterbury Tales*, the host calls upon the main narrator to tell a story. This narrator is, of course, Chaucer himself, who proceeds to tell not one but two tales—that of Sir Thopas and that of Melibeus. In this essay, Trevor Whittock, former lecturer in English at Chancellor College, University of Malawi, explains that these stories are burlesques, or humorous and silly takeoffs on conventional literary styles. Having his own character present them, says Whittock, was Chaucer's way of making that character appear to be a literary "blockhead." Since in his own day Chaucer's readers were perfectly aware that he was anything but stupid, the two tales constitute a sort of literary joke.

No character in the *Canterbury Tales* is more enveloped in irony than the author. As Chaucer portrays himself, this pilgrim is a man of singular stupidity and naïvety. If some lines in the *General Prologue* are to be credited, he is easily taken in by the most obvious rascals. He thinks that the Pardoner is 'in chirche a noble ecclesiaste', and when the Monk sets out his notion of what monks should be and what they should feel free to do the author merely murmurs that 'his opinion was good'. Chaucer the pilgrim disclaims all responsibility for the invention or bawdry of the tales, saying that he merely tried to repeat what was said as closely as he could; and he apologises for not being able to set the Pilgrims down in their proper degree because, 'My wit is short, ye may well understonde'. Naturally the reader finds all this amusing, and enjoys the piquant trick of Chaucer belittling his own shrewdness and artistry. (It must have had even

From *A Reading of "The Canterbury Tales"* by Trevor Whittock. Copyright ©1968 by Cambridge University Press. Reprinted by permission of Cambridge University Press.

more point for the audience to whom Chaucer read his own
poetry: to see the author before them assuming an air of
contrite stupidity.)

A TAKEOFF OF TENTH-RATE LITERATURE

When the Host calls upon Chaucer the pilgrim to tell a tale
the same trick, as we would expect, is exploited further. There
is delight in observing the Host, whom after all Chaucer did
invent (whatever models he may have had), condescendingly
joke about the author's own appearance.... Chaucer, who
has led us to believe that he has sociably talked to all the Pilgrims, and been accepted as one of their company, is here
portrayed by the Host as something of an outsider—a figure
who is so remote within himself that he seems to come from
a different realm. That the Host is apparently unaware of
Chaucer's poetic vocation makes all the more pungent the
mockery of poets for the withdrawn manner they notoriously
affect. The reference to elves in the passage prepares us for
the *Tale of Sir Thopas* with its unreal world that the Host will
find so objectionable. It is a nice touch too that the Host will
finally interrupt Chaucer for being an incompetent versifier,
and abuse him for his foolishness.

The *Tale of Sir Thopas* fits neatly into the joke. So authentic is the burlesque of romances that we can well believe
that Chaucer the pilgrim is unaware how bathetic [ludicrous
and insincere] his doggerel is, and the Host's interruption
comes none too soon. If the *Tale* is slightly boring for the
modern reader for whom the romances parodied are quite
dead, this is the risk any burlesque runs which accurately
takes off the vices of tenth-rate literature which is soon lost
in the whirligig of fashion. There is sufficient absurdity in
the verse, however, for it still to have some life of its own.
... The point of *Sir Thopas* is quickly got. But what are we to
make of the prose tale that follows it?

ANOTHER PAINFUL LEG-PULL?

The *Tale of Melibeus* is an enormous bore, and the bane of
commentators. Some critics merely mutter a soothing nothing before it and hastily pass on to the next tale; others more
openly confess their bafflement or exasperation. The critics
who deal with it are split between those who regard the *Tale
of Melibeus* as another burlesque or painful leg-pull, and
those who regard it as a seriously intended piece of moralis-

ing quite in keeping with the dull homiletics of the time. Let me immediately confess that I am as baffled by it as any of them. Perhaps the best way of expressing the mixed responses this work arouses in me is to give a fictitious biographical account of how Chaucer might have written *Melibeus.*

I imagine that one day Chaucer was approached by an acquaintance who had a low regard for poetry, art or genuine thought, but who wished at times to be informed on matters of fashionable interest. This acquaintance had heard discussed a treatise on consolation and advice, and desired to read it. Having little French or Latin he turned to Chaucer who, while his versifying might not amount to much, was clearly literate and reputed to be a good translator. Chaucer had heard of this work, thought a discussion of prudent forgiveness might be worth studying, and agreed to make the translation. When he came to work on it, however, he found it to be quite preposterous.

A man called Melibeus returns home to find that foes have attacked and wounded his daughter in five different parts of her body. Desiring revenge, he calls for counsel. First he hearkens to flatterers . . . but his wife soon sets him right. Most of the tale in fact consists of the debate between Melibeus and Dame Prudence in which not only does she do most of the talking but what she says is invariably right, and recognised to be so by her husband. But all this is not to be read too literally, as the tale is really an allegory: Melibeus' daughter is his heart; the three foes are the flesh, the fiend, and the world; the five wounds are the five senses through which the foes enter; and Dame Prudence is the wiser part of Melibeus' reason. She counsels reconciliation rather than revenge. Through her timely intervention, Melibeus forgives the three foes and takes them to his grace, as he trusts God will do to all men. What happens to the daughter is not made clear, but doubtless she recovers.

Perhaps such a tale could have made a powerful piece of didactic writing: but this, Chaucer soon found, was not the case here. To succeed, the conventions holding the tale together would have to be skilfully controlled. Instead reality and symbol, humanity and preaching were ineptly juxtaposed. But even more disastrous than this and what most struck Chaucer with his sensitive feeling for language, was the tale's ridiculous overabundance of proverbs. But he had agreed to translate it, and he began by trying to make the best of a bad job. Some parts of it, whole paragraphs even, he could render lucidly and forcefully.... But the material as a whole defeated serious adaptation. Chaucer realised that as it stood it was a monument to misguided purpose and inept craftsmanship. Hence he was all the more amused to find that his patron, who so despised Chaucer's finest poetry, praised this work and its translator.

How *Not* to Present an Argument

In time a mischievous idea took root in Chaucer's mind. Why not incorporate it in the *Canterbury Tales* as the tale he himself tells? What could more fittingly illustrate the fumblings of the uninspired *litterateur* he was portraying himself to be? What could more mockingly settle the score with those in his audience wanting in all literary judgment, particularly as they would not even recognise any mockery at all? Furthermore, some of the arguments in the tale would fit in quite well with themes in *Canterbury Tales*. *The Physician's Tale* deals with a father whose daughter is wronged, and *The Prioress's Tale* touches upon the vengeance wrought upon the Jews for killing the little child. At least *Melibeus* will draw people into reconsidering the rightness of vengeance. The unreal debate between husband and wife in *Melibeus* could also be used to good effect by contrasting it with the Wife of Bath's monologues directed at her husbands. To bring this out Chaucer deliberately develops the argument on the merits of women, and lets Dame Prudence at one stage use the very same words as the Wife of Bath.... The sweet eloquence(!) of Dame Prudence also can cause the Host to contrast her with his own wife, and so introduce a touch of comedy not unrelated to the 'marriage debate'.

Chaucer further hoped, I surmise, by including this tale to make the perceptive reader appreciate a writer's difficulty in organising his material. For a writer, one of his crucial problems is how to direct and control his reader's responses, and one of the important methods he has at his disposal is the employment of recognised *conventions*. He has to eschew [avoid] matter alien to the convention he selects, or so modify it that it will not conflict with the basic unfolding of his subject. Where he mixes two or more conventions he has to be even more careful, lest the shift from one to another leads the reader to misapprehend the tone or purport of parts of the work. Since Chaucer himself was in the habit of juggling with many conventions in one work, he must have been particularly aware of the risks entailed. Where a writer, through ineptitude or bad craftsmanship, muddles his conventions, the reader is disconcerted to find extraneous and contradictory notions entering into his reading, and he doubts the writer's argument even while it is unfolding. Perhaps Chaucer, recognising that this is exactly what the inept construction of *Melibeus* resulted in, attempted to turn it into good use by making it a model of how *not* to present an argument. Thus he deliberately permitted the 'naturalism' in *Melibeus* clumsily to jostle the allegory, and encouraged the human situation of marital discussion to throw off-balance the allegorical debate. . . .

THE READER SNORES

Further, a writer must know when to prune and avoid excess. A literary device overdone loses its effectiveness. But Chaucer makes no attempt to stop the flow of proverbs in *Melibeus:* on the contrary he lets them pile up till the effect is preposterous, and the reader, now impatient with proverbs and their shifting uses, grows completely sceptical of their application. Only a blockhead could write so badly, and that is exactly how Chaucer wished to portray himself as a pilgrim. . . . *Melibeus* is merely his caricature of himself as a stodgy and tedious adapter. Perhaps his very desire to distinguish his false shadow from his real art betrayed him into dragging out *Melibeus* so interminably.

Partly by means of the suppositious [speculative] account of how Chaucer came to write and include the tale, I have tried to present my mixed responses to this work with its earnestness of theme and its un-Chaucerian dullness of performance. But whatever its purpose, *Melibeus* to my mind is not a success. I cannot be grateful for its inclusion in the *Canterbury Tales.* One critic has remarked of Chaucer's work, 'No doubt Chaucer nodded like all other artists, but I think he did not often snore'. Whether he did or not here is debatable, but (to twist the 'sentence') I suspect many a reader faced with this tale has snored.

The *Pardoner's Tale:* A Quest for Death

Michael Hoy

The Pardoner is widely viewed as one of the most colorful and interesting characters in *The Canterbury Tales* and his tale is certainly among the most famous and dramatic. In this excerpt from his book *Chaucer's Major Tales*, Michael Hoy, a well-known scholar of and writer about English literature, addresses the qualities of both the character and the tale. Regarding the Pardoner himself, Hoy proposes that this extraordinarily well drawn character personifies Chaucer's ability to create a "dualism" in his characters; that is, the Pardoner is a wonderfully rendered example of a familiar general character type, and at the same time a realistic, rounded, and believable individual personality. Hoy also includes an analysis of the tale itself, an unforgettable account of greed and death, in which he explains how Chaucer uses detail to create realism and the rhythm of the lines to heighten the excitement and suspense.

During the last centuries of the Middle Ages there arose a deep and macabre obsession with death. In *The Waning of the Middle Ages*, J. Huizinga points out how all-pervasive was the primitive and terrifying image of death which intensified as so much of the structure of medieval life began to crumble:

> No other epoch [historical era] has laid so much stress as the expiring Middle Ages on the thought of death. An everlasting call of *memento mori* [remember that you must die] resounds through life. Denis the Carthusian, in his *Directory of the Life of Nobles*, exhorts them: 'And when going to bed at night, he should consider how, just as he now lies down himself, soon strange hands will lay his body in the grave.'

The conception of death was crude and direct. It had to be,

From *Chaucer's Major Tales* by Michael Hoy and Michael Stevens. Copyright ©1969 by Michael Hoy and Michael Stevens. Reprinted by permission of Schocken Books, published by Pantheon Books, a division of Random House, Inc.

since so much of the complex thought of earlier centuries was entirely unsuited to the unsophisticated techniques of forms like the sermon and the popular woodcut, media through which the idea of death was communicated. And it is because the images are so direct and primitive that the vision had such an impact on medieval life. In the late Middle Ages, the elegiac approach of lamentation for the passing of former glories diminished in importance. Instead, attention focused more and more on the motif of physical decay of the human body. Terrifying visual representation of the spectacle of decomposition was frequent in tomb carvings and paintings. This we may find in the horrific images in the churchyard of the Innocents at Paris, for example, and in the poetry of François Villon. Also represented pictorially in woodcuts, sculpture, frescoes and other forms was a third idea, the Dance of Death. The force of this image lay in the identification of living men with the inevitable fact of death, for the vision was of an actual dancing *body* carrying off men; the image did not become a skeleton until late in the fifteenth century with [German painter Hans] Holbein's 'Dance of Death'. These ideas, which were widely expressed in art and literature, used and increased medieval man's fear of death. The church in turn played upon the obsession and used it to further moral arguments. And so we find that the vision of death occupies a major place in medieval sermons.

The obsessive vision of death took on a new and terrible aspect in the late summer of 1348, when the Black Death reached the southern ports of England and began to ravage the land and its people. Throughout the year, the rat-borne bubonic plague had been spreading swiftly through Europe from the Black Sea, leaving in its wake a trail of desolation. In England the first epidemic alone carried off at least one third of the population, and all grew to fear the sinister symptoms of infection, the black boils and delirious agony. Here, it seemed, was a Dance of Death which would only end with the total destruction of mankind. And so ... the plague took on the aspect of an apocalyptic sign, interpreted by many as a token of God's wrath and vengeance on a sinful people.

Yet the moral exhortations of the religious failed to halt the pestilence. The church itself, in fact, became one of the chief victims of the social and economic collapse consequent on the plague. Many religious houses lost all their wealth, and the Black Death carried off the very men needed for their reconstruction. The life of common men was affected even more, as harvests rotted unreaped in the fields around empty villages, and cattle wandered untended and dying. . . . Medieval life was totally disrupted, and the religious and social structure of England largely collapsed.

THE REPULSIVE AND HYPOCRITICAL PARDONER

It is against this background that we must set the tale of death and damnation which the Pardoner tells to the Canterbury pilgrims. The Pardoner is the last of the pilgrims to be described in 'The General Prologue'. Like the Summoner, with whom he rides as a close companion, the Pardoner is given a full and detailed portrait. . . .

CHAUCER DESCRIBES THE PARDONER

The following excerpt from The Canterbury Tales *appears in the translation by Vincent F. Hopper.*

With him there rode a gentle PARDONER
Of Rouncivalle, his friend and comrade,
Who had come straight from the court of Rome.
Full loudly he sang, "Come hither, love, to me."
The summoner joined him with a stiff bass,
Never was there trumpet half so powerful.
This pardoner had hair as yellow as wax
But smooth it hung, as does a hank of flax,
Such locks as he had hung down thinly,
And with them he covered his shoulders;
But sparsely it lay, by shreds here and there;
Yet, for amusement, he wore no hood,
For it was packed in his bag.
He thought he rode in the latest style;
Dishevelled and bareheaded except for his cap.
He had glistening eyes like a hare's.
He had a veronica[1] sewed on his cap.
His bag lay before him on his lap,
Crammed with pardons brought from Rome all hot.
A voice he had as tiny as a goat's.
No beard had he, nor ever would have,
As smooth he was as if he'd just shaved;
I believe he was a gelding or a mare.

1. a handkerchief supposedly bearing the imprint of Christ's face

[The Pardoner and Summoner] are singing together a love-song, something which immediately strikes a note discordant with their ecclesiastical situations. This sense of incongruity grows stronger as the description proceeds. The Pardoner follows the latest trends in fashion, or so he thinks . . . , and his deliberate jauntiness associates him with the secular life. He is further distanced from his calling by his appearance. He is physically repugnant, although he does not have the openly frightening appearance of the Summoner. Yet there is something more subtly repulsive about the Pardoner. His appearance is effeminate, with long fair hair and staring eyes. . . . His soft, high-pitched, bleating voice and his smooth complexion emphasize this, and Chaucer sums up the total effect with an image of sexual impotence taken from the rural scene [calling the Pardoner a gelding, or a castrated horse]. . . . These features show clearly that Chaucer's Pardoner is an eunuch [a man whose sex organs have been removed]. . . .

The second part of Chaucer's introductory description of the Pardoner concerns his activities in his office. This forms a striking parallel with the previous details of his physical characteristics, for here again there is a strong sense of delusion and emptiness. Physically the Pardoner is not what he seems. His hair may be fair and long, but it is thin and matted, and his attempt to follow fashion in his clothing is a mockery. His attitude to his ecclesiastical position is similar, since it is based wholly on deceit and hypocrisy. Poor, ignorant folk who take advantage of his services merely fill his pockets with their hard-earned savings, and, of course, he has no interest at all in their spiritual welfare. . . . There is an insidious and sinister evil in the Pardoner which Chaucer clearly conveys in this initial portrait, and yet, at the same time, we are aware of another side to our attitude to the rogue. For he is also a figure of high comedy. . . .

A FIGURE OF COMEDY AND EVIL

From the outset, then, Chaucer calls forth from us a dual response to his Pardoner. He is at once a figure of comedy and of sinister evil. This is a fundamental feature of Chaucer's design, for it produces a character who is both a type and a full and rounded personality. . . . By the fourteenth century false pardoners similar to Chaucer's character could be found throughout England. There is a great deal of evidence to support this, not only in historical documents, but also in works of literature such as the satirical description of a pardoner in William Langland's *Piers Plowman*. So Chaucer has not drawn an exaggerated picture of an unreal villain. On the contrary, both he and his contemporaries must have been very familiar with such manifestations of the widespread corruption of the church in the later Middle Ages.

Although he briefly interrupts the Wife of Bath with a blatant but amusing lie, the Pardoner does not hold the stage again until he is invited by Harry Bailly to dispel the gloom created by the Physician's Tale of false justice and cruel murder. Harry Bailly clearly wants a bawdy *fabliau* [comic] story, and the Pardoner, despite his ecclesiastical office, appears to be quite ready to oblige. But he is forestalled by the 'gentils', who demand a more constructive and 'honest' Tale.... To this the Pardoner readily agrees, and, provided with a glass of ale and a cake, he proceeds with his Prologue....

THE PARDONER AS A PREACHER

From the start we see the Pardoner as a preacher, and we are at once reminded of the concluding lines of his portrait in 'The General Prologue'. Preaching he loves, and it is an art in which he is highly skilled. In these opening lines the compelling drama of his style is conveyed through the urgent rhythm of the verse, and we are immediately captivated by his roguish boasting and self-confidence. It is a technique which he has used to his own advantage for many years, successfully manipulating his unfortunate congregations to fill his pockets. Preaching, however, was the task of the priest, and not of lay officers of the church. Lay pardoners were therefore not permitted to preach. Yet Chaucer's Pardoner appears to be a layman, and so his whole position is illegal. But the church's legislation concerning such activities was ineffectual. In addition to preaching it attempted to exercise some sort of control over the practice of selling pardons by issuing licences to its appointed officers. Chaucer's Pardoner possesses such a licence, and he tells the pilgrims that he shows this official permit wherever he preaches in order to establish his authority.... But the Pardoner is not content with this bishop's seal alone. He has a variety of other documents, probably forged, which he uses to deceive his congregation....

He turns now to the bones and pieces of cloth which he

carries in glass containers, holy relics with beneficial powers. That they are useless fakes the Pardoner knows full well. ... [He] has nothing but contempt for the poor, ignorant souls who are completely taken in by his practices, although these are the people who provide him with a living. ...

BLASPHEMY WORSE THAN MURDER?

The Pardoner's Prologue takes the form of a confession, a deliberate revelation of motives and techniques. This device was a common convention in medieval literature, and ... also the device which Chaucer employs with such skill in the Wife of Bath's Prologue to her Tale. It is important to recognize that this conventional framework lies behind Chaucer's approach. It is, at the same time, highly appropriate to the Pardoner whose self-confident pride demands an outlet of confessional exhibitionism. There is, of course, much more to the Pardoner's Prologue than a simple medieval convention. Chaucer has combined with this a wealth of realistic detail, and he has presented the whole structure through fast-moving dramatic speech which forces us to listen to the performer. Such a man as the Pardoner must of necessity boast of his skill and gloat over the misfortunes of his unfortunate victims. And indeed he does so with such vigour that we are completely absorbed by the spectacle. We may wish at times to rise up in indignation and pass moral censure on the villain, but at the same time we are prevented by his hypnotic power. ...

The Pardoner begins his Tale with a detailed account of the sins indulged by the young men of Flanders. The description is realistic in its technique, for we have a striking picture of the gamblers and dancing-girls, of the strident noise and whirling movements. Yet there is more to this scene-setting than would appear at first sight. The whole description is coloured by the personality of the Pardoner. He betrays a certain fascination for the horrors of the immorality with which he is concerned, although this is clearly accompanied by a tone of moral indignation. This fascination is conveyed through the accuracy and immediacy of the details of the account. ... It is also recreated in the violence of the rhythm. We can hear his voice rising in pitch through the first eight lines until, with a gasping emphasis, the syntax brings him to a halt on the long, important words 'superfluytee abhomynable' [abominable excesses]. The tone of moral indignation which balances the Pardoner's interest in the details of sin is found in the imagery of this opening verse paragraph. The idea that sin is a direct and active opposition to God is clearly expressed in the transformation of the tavern into a temple where the Devil is worshipped by the young sinners. . . . This is followed by a more specific instance in the traditional medieval idea that swearing tore apart the body of Christ and crucified him again. . . .

Both these sins which the Pardoner discusses with such relish are forms of blasphemy. Swearing is clearly verbal blasphemy, and no less blasphemous is the worship of the devil in the tavern sins. Blasphemy is a major theme in the Tale, especially in the Sermon Digression, and the Pardoner considers it to be the worst of all sins. . . . To say that blasphemy is a sin worse than murder because it comes earlier in the prohibitions of the Ten Commandments is typical of the imaginative way in which the Pardoner uses the Scriptures and ecclesiastical ideas. The idea has a special significance for the human comedy among the pilgrims, since this is a sly attack on Harry Bailly whose vigorously emotional response to 'The Physician's Tale' included many examples of blasphemous swearing. . . .

FUSING ALL SINS TOGETHER

But the Pardoner's idea has a more important function than this. Throughout his Tale he is concerned to show the interconnection between all sins. He is, of course, absorbed by the details of individual sins, but his main purpose is to show how great and terrifying is sin by fusing all sins together to produce a magnification of evil. He begins to stress the interconnection of sins at the beginning of the Sermon Digression. . . . Gluttony and lechery are closely related, a fact which the Pardoner illustrates with two highly appropriate references. The first is a reference to Saint Paul's Letter to Ephesians, although Chaucer's medieval meaning of the word 'luxurie' is more specifically *sexual* excess, as opposed to Paul's more general meaning (*luxuria*—excess). The second refers to the biblical story of Lot, who was led to commit incestuous sin by excess of wine. Later in the sermon gluttony is again fused with the greater sin of blasphemy. Similarly, the Pardoner's attack on gambling begins with a list of other sins which are closely interconnected. . . . And the conclusion of the whole digression brings the various sins together once again, and fuses them within the greater unity of the idea of blasphemy. . . .

This, then, is the Pardoner's overall design in the Sermon Digression. It provides unity within the variety of the sins and illustrations in the homily and, more important, it serves to link the digression with the actual Tale of the three revellers. Some commentators have seen little connection at all between the digression on sin and the Tale itself, but Chaucer has established a positive structural link. The revellers, who begin their quest for Death in a tavern, are guilty of all the sins which the Pardoner condemns in his sermon. In their Tale the fusion of the sins of gluttony, gambling and murder creates a larger evil similar in dimensions to the combined blasphemy of the sins of the homily. Their avarice is therefore magnified by its inclusion within a wider and darker vision of sin, blasphemy itself. . . .

The effect is hypnotic. At the same time it is highly entertaining. The subject matter of the sermon is skilfully varied, and so too is his compelling style, with its combination of high rhetoric and low, coarse colloquialisms, of sombre biblical reference and the fast rhythms of exciting narrative. He is outstandingly successful as preacher and entertainer, and even if he cannot convince the wily Harry Bailly, there will be many other simple folk who will continue to be taken in by the villain's tricks and furnish him with his handsome annual income.

ON A FRUITLESS QUEST

When at last we return to the Tale, the Pardoner plunges right into the heart of the story. It is of no consequence that the 'riotoures thre' [three rioters] have not been mentioned previously in the Tale. This sort of continuity is not important, and the Pardoner is obviously not aiming to provide a continuous logical thread. We have only to see how he jumps from one style to another and from one subject or *exemplum* to the next to realize this. To criticize Chaucer on the grounds that he is inconsistent is to misunderstand an important feature of the Pardoner's character. He is always master of his material, and he is prepared to use anything for his own ends, however illogical his transitions may be.

The language of the narrative itself is simple and the verse moves at a great pace. Chaucer's technique is marked by careful selection of details, such as the tinkling of the bell in the funeral procession, and at once we are present at the scene, and involved in the ensuing dialogue.... The violent rhythms of the dialogue, punctuated by blasphemous oaths, continue until the three rioters have pledged themselves in brotherhood in their search for Death.... In accordance with the obsessive medieval vision of Death, it is a real person whom they set out to find and kill. This brings into the narrative the idea of a quest, which is a key feature of the structure of the Tale. And it is the concrete reality of Chaucer's adaptation of the conventional personification of death which gives to the quest its drama and immediacy.

Eventually, of course, the revellers reach the end of their quest, but the death they meet is not in the form of a person. They do, however, meet a person during their search, the Old Man who is engaged on the same quest for Death as they are. Who is the Old Man in the Tale? There have been many answers to this question. Some readers have seen the Old Man as an allegory of Death itself, and at first sight there would appear to be some truth in this view. Within the quest for the person of Death, this figure is the sole person encountered by the revellers. What is more, his closing remarks show quite clearly that he knows a great deal about Death—even where he may be found. In contrast to this, however, there is the basic incongruity that the Old Man is himself engaged in a fruitless search for Death. Chaucer must intend us to associate the Old Man with Death, but a specific allegorical reading merely confuses the meaning of the Tale. There is much more to the Old Man than a conventional personification of Death....

Chaucer's portrait of the Old Man is deliberately full of suggestion. An air of dark mystery surrounds him, and although the source of this feeling is not made specific, Chaucer clearly invites us to associate him with a variety of figures and meanings. Indeed, this lack of explanation makes the Old Man a most powerful force in the Tale. Yet at the same time he is a real person. Chaucer's description and, more important, the dialogue present to us a picture of an old man tired of life, wishing to die since no young man will exchange his youth for old age.... We begin to feel a strong sense that the Old Man is not all that he seems. The revellers share this, and they are led to accuse him of being Death's spy. Thus from the initial apparent insignificance of the Old Man we become aware of an increasing air of mystery. We begin to ask questions about the the Old Man, not only who he is, but where he has come from and where he is going. This response is exactly what Chaucer's design in the Tale demands, and it is for this reason that he refuses to give any specific explanations as to the Old Man's identity. The questions are never answered. As the young revellers rush off to find Death beneath the oak tree, the Old Man walks out of the Tale as mysteriously as he entered it. . . .

GREED LEADS TO TRAGEDY

The brief, speedy narrative of the discovery of the treasure by the three revellers is a marked contrast to the preceding dialogue. In the space of a mere eight lines the whole situation and movement of the Tale is completely changed, and the significance of this new development Chaucer has compressed into a single line: 'No lenger thanne after Deeth they soughte' ["No longer did they search for death"]. But its true significance is not immediately apparent. It is only during the ensuing dialogue that we recognize a powerful irony in this statement. The opening words of the worst of the revellers ["Fortune has given us this treasure"] are doubly ironic. . . .

The irony lies primarily in the fact that the first villain begins to play on the mind of the second by appealing to the very qualities of brotherhood and loyalty which bind all three together. We notice how the repetition of the pronoun 'thou' serves to exclude the youngest reveller from the oath sworn in the tavern, and to strengthen the ties between the other two. . . . The brief, simple questions of the second reveller reveal not only a misunderstanding of his companion's purposed but also a certain wariness. He obviously senses that something is wrong, but he is not prepared to take the initiative. This has the effect of increasing the suspense, and the tension mounts as it becomes necessary for the instigator of the plot to reveal exactly what he intends. And so Chaucer leads him to a breathless account of his plans, in which the excitement of the conspiracy comes through the verse in the fast-moving syntax and the repetition of the conjunction 'and'. No sooner have they pledged themselves to murder the youngest reveller than Chaucer deftly accomplishes a change of focus. The effect of the conspiracy has been to throw our sympathy onto the victim of the plot, but this is short-lived. In a striking image of the golden coins actually rolling about in the young reveller's imagination,

Chaucer shows that he too is preoccupied with the prospect of wealth, and we find that he is just like his companions.

The narrative of his purchase of the poison and his conversation with the apothecary offers a particularly good example of Chaucer's imagination at work. The apothecary may ask why the young reveller needs the poison, and thus Chaucer creates the excellent idea of the rats and the polecat. The details bring this whole sequence dramatically alive. We take special note of the apothecary's knowledgeable account of the swift effect of the poison, and the brief description of the three large bottles into which the poison is poured. Careful selection of detail creates realism and also a simplicity of style which contributes a great deal to the terrifying sense of inevitability which invests the tale as it approaches its climax.

The final outcome of the Tale [in which the men kill one another] is narrated in a deliberately flat style.... Here the pace of the narrative becomes even quicker, and it is as though we are watching the revellers rush grotesquely into the arms of Death. And so the Tale moves at great speed to its conclusion, and ironically it is the very end which the villains set out to find on their quest....

THE PARDONER DAMNED TOO

The final irony of the Tale lies in the Pardoner's invitation to Harry Bailly to come forward and be absolved. For although the Pardoner clearly shows with what skill he can manipulate the thoughts and emotions of his congregation, his power is limited. Harry Bailly is not deceived by him, and this the Pardoner fails to recognize. He has deceived himself into a belief that no one can resist his preaching. This is but one small aspect of the total self-deception which we find in the Pardoner. Although we come to recognize this self-deception in the sermon, we cannot fully comprehend its causes, for the Pardoner remains a figure of paradox and, above all, of irony. The irony does not only lie in the fact that he is successful in moving sinners to repentance. There is irony in his own predicament, for just as the three revellers fail to understand that the wages of sin is death, so the Pardoner never sees that he is condemned according to his own terms. It is true that he fully recognizes his own hypocrisy. He is guilty of the sin of avarice, and that, according to his text, is the root of all evils. What he fails to realize is the full significance of those evils and the damnation which they imply and which is the inevitable consequence of them. He can describe in vivid and dramatic terms the process of sin and its results, and he takes us in his Tale to the very brink of damnation. But he fails to see any connection between this process and his own situation; he is blind to the fact that the quest of the Tale is his own quest.

CHRONOLOGY

1327

Edward III ascends the English throne

1337

Outbreak of the so-called Hundred Years' War between England and France

CA. 1340

Geoffrey Chaucer is born, probably in London

1346

The English defeat the French at Crécy

1348–1349

The bubonic plague, known as the Black Death, sweeps through England, killing thousands

1349

Chaucer begins attending London's St. Paul's Cathedral School

1356

The English are victorious at Poitiers; France's King Jean is captured and held under house arrest in London

1357

Chaucer becomes a page in the household of Lionel, earl of Ulster, second son of Edward III

1359–1360

Chaucer fights as a soldier against the French in the Hundred Years' War; he is taken prisoner during the siege of Reims but ransomed soon afterward

1360

Edward III and King Jean sign the Treaty of Brétigny; halting hostilities between England and France

1366

Chaucer marries Philippa Roet, a lady-in-waiting to the queen; his father dies

CA. 1367

Chaucer begins writing his first important work, *The Book of the Duchess*

1367

Chaucer is drafted into the king's service as a civil servant and diplomat, specifically as Esquire of the Royal Household, and awarded a salary for life

1369

England and France resume hostilities

1372–1373

Chaucer travels to Italy, first negotiating the use of an English port by a Genoese merchant fleet, and then arranging loans in Florence; the trip introduces him to Renaissance Italy and he is influenced by the works of Dante, Boccaccio, and Petrarch

1377

Richard II becomes king of England; the new king confirms Chaucer's offices and salary

1381

Chaucer's mother dies; his son Lewis is born

1381–1386

Chaucer composes one of his greatest works, *Troilus and Criseyde*, based on the ancient Greek legend of the Trojan War

1381

King Richard puts down a "peasants' revolt" led by Walter Tyler

1382

King Richard marries Anne of Bohemia

1386–1388

First phase of the creation of Chaucer's masterpiece, *The Canterbury Tales*, including the General Prologue and the *Knight's Tale*

1387

Philippa Chaucer dies; Chaucer goes on a diplomatic mission to France

1389

Chaucer is appointed Clerk of the Works, in charge of maintaining the Tower of London and other government buildings

1389–1396

Second phase of the *Tales*, including the tales of the Wife of Bath, Merchant, and Friar

1394

Queen Anne dies

1396–1400

Third phase of the *Tales*, including the tales of the Canon's Yeoman, Manciple, and Pardoner

1399

Richard II is deposed by Henry of Bolingbroke; Henry ascends the throne as Henry IV

1400

A conspiracy to restore Richard II to the throne fails; Richard is murdered while under arrest; Chaucer dies and is buried in London's Westminster Abbey, initiating what will become famous as the Poet's Corner

WORKS BY GEOFFREY CHAUCER

Note: Chaucer left some works unfinished and worked intermittently on others over periods of several years; also, very little of a definite nature is known about his life. Consequently, the exact dates on which he began and completed many works are uncertain and must be approximated.

Early poems, including "An ABC," few of which have survived (ca. 1360–1368)

The Book of the Duchess begun (1366)

The House of Fame begun (1374)

Translation of Boethius's *Consolation of Philosophy* (ca. 1380)

Translation of Pope Innocent III's *On the Misery of the Human Condition* (ca. 1380)

Translation of Albertanus of Brescia's *Book of Consolation and Counsel* (scholars differ on whether this is Chaucer's) (ca. 1380)

The Parliament of Fowls completed (1380)

Troilus and Criseyde (1381–1386)

The Legend of Good Women begun (1386)

The Canterbury Tales begun (1386)

Treatise on the Astrolabe (1391–1392)

FOR FURTHER RESEARCH

EDITIONS OF *THE CANTERBURY TALES* AND OTHER WORKS BY CHAUCER

Nevill Coghill, trans., *The Canterbury Tales*, by Geoffrey Chaucer. London: Penguin Books, 1977.

——, *The Canterbury Tales, An Illustrated Edition*, by Geoffrey Chaucer. London: Cresset, 1986.

Barbara Cohen, ed. and trans., *Canterbury Tales*, by Geoffrey Chaucer. New York: Lothrop, Lee and Shepard, 1988. *Editor's note:* Ms. Cohen has here translated selected tales into a simplified prose narrative suitable for young readers.

E.T. Donaldson, ed., *Chaucer's Poetry: An Anthology for the Modern Reader.* New York: Ronald Press, 1975.

Ronald L. Ecker and Eugene J. Crook, trans., *The Canterbury Tales*, by Geoffrey Chaucer. Palatka, FL: Hodge and Braddock, 1993.

John H. Fisher, ed., *The Complete Poetry and Prose of Geoffrey Chaucer.* New York: Holt, Rinehart, and Winston, 1977.

Vincent F. Hopper, trans., *Chaucer's Canterbury Tales (Selected): An Interlinear Translation.* Great Neck, NY: Barron's Educational Series, 1948.

Donald R. Howard and James Dean, eds., *The Canterbury Tales: A Selection.* New York: Signet, 1969.

J.U. Nicolson, trans., *Canterbury Tales*, by Geoffrey Chaucer. New York: Garden City Publishing, 1934.

F.N. Robinson, ed., *The Works of Geoffrey Chaucer.* Boston: Houghton Mifflin, 1957. *Editor's note:* This is the most often quoted and studied of modern Chaucer translations.

Eva March Tappan, *The Chaucer Story Book.* Boston: Houghton Mifflin, 1908. *Editor's note:* Ms. Tappan has here translated selected sections of *The Canterbury Tales* into a simplified prose narrative. Though old, it is hardly dated.

ABOUT *THE CANTERBURY TALES*

Malcom Andrew, *Critical Essays on Chaucer's Canterbury Tales.* Toronto: University of Toronto Press, 1991.

Harold Bloom, ed., *Modern Critical Interpretations of Geoffrey Chaucer's "The Knight's Tale."* New York: Chelsea House, 1988.

Muriel Bowden, *A Commentary on the General Prologue to The Canterbury Tales.* New York: Macmillan, 1967.

Helen Cooper, *Oxford Guides to Chaucer: The Canterbury Tales.* Oxford: Oxford University Press, 1989.

Margaret Hallissy, *A Companion to Chaucer's Canterbury Tales.* Westport, CT: Greenwood Press, 1995. *Editor's note:* This is the most comprehensive and up-to-date general companion to the *Tales* presently available.

Richard L. Hoffman, *Ovid and The Canterbury Tales.* London: Oxford University Press, 1966.

Donald R. Howard, *The Idea of The Canterbury Tales.* Berkeley and Los Angeles: University of California Press, 1976.

Michael Hoy and Michael Stevens, *Chaucer's Major Tales.* London: Norton Bailey, 1969.

R.M. Lumiansky, *Of Sondry Folk: The Dramatic Principle in The Canterbury Tales.* Austin: University of Texas Press, 1955.

Trevor Whittock, *A Reading of the Canterbury Tales.* Cambridge, England: Cambridge University Press, 1968.

Also see the quarterly issues of the *Chaucer Review* (published by the Pennsylvania State University Press) for continuing debate and discussion of various aspects of *The Canterbury Tales.*

ABOUT CHAUCER, HIS WORKS, AND HIS WORLD

Harold Bloom, ed., *Geoffrey Chaucer: Modern Critical Views.* New York: Chelsea House, 1985.

Piero Boitani and Jill Mann, eds., *The Cambridge Chaucer Companion.* Cambridge, England: Cambridge University Press, 1986.

Derek Brewer, *Chaucer and His World.* London: Eyre Methuen, 1978.

David Burnley, *The Language of Chaucer.* London: Macmillan, 1983.

Marchette Chute, *Geoffrey Chaucer of England.* New York: E.P. Dutton, 1946.

Norman Davis et al., *A Chaucer Glossary.* Oxford: Clarendon Press, 1979.

James M. Dean and Christian K. Zacher, eds., *The Idea of Medieval Literature: New Essays on Chaucer and Medieval Culture in Honor of Donald R. Howard.* Newark: University of Delaware Press, 1992.

George D. Economou, ed., *Geoffrey Chaucer: A Collection of Original Articles.* New York: McGraw-Hill, 1975.

John Gardner, *The Life and Times of Chaucer.* New York: Knopf, 1977.

M.W. Grose, *Chaucer.* New York: Arco Publishing, 1969.

Elaine T. Hansen, *Chaucer and the Fictions of Gender.* Berkeley and Los Angeles: University of California Press, 1992.

Gertrude Hartman, *Medieval Days and Ways.* New York: Macmillan, 1960.

Donald R. Howard, *Chaucer: His Life, His Works, His World.* New York: Dutton, 1987.

Maurice Hussey, *Chaucer's World: A Pictorial Companion.* Cambridge, England: Cambridge University Press, 1967.

Maurice Hussey et al., *An Introduction to Chaucer.* Cambridge, England: Cambridge University Press, 1965.

Harry A. Kelly, *Love and Marriage in the Age of Chaucer.* Ithaca, NY: Cornell University Press, 1975.

Helge Kokeritz, *A Guide to Chaucer's Pronunciation.* Toronto: University of Toronto Press, 1978.

Roger S. Loomis, *A Mirror of Chaucer's World.* Princeton: Princeton University Press, 1965.

Priscilla Martin, *Chaucer's Women: Nuns, Wives, and Amazons.* Iowa City: University of Iowa Press, 1990.

Robert P. Miller, ed., *Chaucer: Sources and Backgrounds.* New York: Oxford University Press, 1977.

Eileen Power, *Medieval People.* New York: Barnes and Noble, 1963.

George Williams, *A New View of Chaucer.* Durham, NC: Duke University Press, 1965.

Also see the quarterly issues of the *Chaucer Review* (published by the Pennsylvania State University Press) for continuing debate and discussion of various works by Chaucer, as well as new research and information about his life and society.

INDEX